OXFORD MEDICAL PUBLICATIONS

Epilepsy

THE FACTS

Epilepsy

THE FACTS

ANTHONY HOPKINS

*Physician in Charge, Department of Neurological Sciences,
St. Bartholomew's Hospital, London.*

OXFORD
OXFORD UNIVERSITY PRESS
NEW YORK TORONTO
1981

Oxford University Press, Walton Street, Oxford OX2 6DP

London Glasgow New York Toronto
Delhi Bombay Calcutta Madras Karachi
Kuala Lumpur Singapore Hong Kong Tokyo
Nairobi Dar es Salaam Cape Town
Melbourne Wellington

and associate companies in
Beirut Berlin Ibadan Mexico City

British Library Cataloguing in Publication Data
Hopkins, Anthony
    Epilepsy. – (Oxford medical publications)
    1. Epilepsy
    I. Title
    616.85'3   RC372
    ISBN 0-19-261257-3

Typset by Hope Services, Abingdon
Printed in Great Britain by
Richard Clay (The Chaucer Press) Ltd,
Bungay, Suffolk

Preface

There are more misunderstandings about epilepsy than perhaps any other illness except cancer. Epileptic seizures are common. At any one time about 1 in 200 of the population will be on medical treatment for epilepsy that is more or less active. Every day 65 people in the United Kingdom have their first seizure. Many readers will have seen friends or strangers having seizures, and not known what they should do. This feeling of incompetence is reinforced by misconceptions that people with epilepsy are somehow 'different', that there is some relationship between epilepsy and mental insufficiency, that epilepsy invariably begins in childhood and never stops, and that epilepsy will be passed on to the next generation. It is the purpose of this book to dispel such misconceptions.

It is not possible to write about any illness without using some technical terms, but I have explained each term as it first appears, and reference to the index will allow the reader to seek the definitions again if necessary.

Some information, such as the numbers of those with epilepsy, and the law on eligibility to hold a driving licence, refers only to the United Kingdom. Nevertheless there is much common ground in the management of epilepsy throughout the world, and I hope that readers in all English-speaking countries will find this book useful. Specific information on legal aspects in other countries can be obtained from national Epilepsy Associations or branches of the International League Against Epilepsy.

Neurologists (doctors who specialize in physical disorders of the functions of the brain, as opposed to psychiatrists who specialize in psychological illnesses) have a better understanding of epilepsy than most. They spend a considerable proportion of their professional lives treating and advising about seizures. They are specialists in this field, and this knowledge is not shared by all doctors. In my experience misunderstandings between doctors and patients with epilepsy are common, especially as a diagnosis of epilepsy may result in a lost job or a lost driving licence. I believe that a full understanding of epilepsy by the subject and his family is the backbone of successful management. I hope this book helps people with epilepsy, and leads to a better understanding of their problems by those without epilepsy.

9 Upper Wimpole Street   Anthony Hopkins
London W1.   March 1981

Acknowledgements

I am grateful to Dr W. A. Hauser and Dr L. T. Kurland and the publisher of *Epilepsia* to reproduce the information shown in Figure 3, to Dr F. Annegers and his co-authors and the same publisher for their permission to reproduce the information shown in Figure 13, and to Professor W.B. Jennett and Heinemann books for their permission to reproduce Figure 8. I am also grateful to my colleague Dr William Cobb for providing the electroencephalograms for Figures 10–12.

Graham Scambler was Research Associate on the survey of epilepsy in Metropolitan London, discussed at several places in this book.

Contents

1

What is epilepsy?

How nerve cells work

The human brain contains about 100 000 million nerve cells called neurones, each of which is connected to many others — perhaps as many as 50 000 others. The brain is the organ of our thinking, and of our memory. It integrates information from the outside world and so allows us to perceive objects and events around us. It organizes our response to these events by movements or other action. It organizes our social behaviour. Figure 1 shows the main areas of the brain that are mentioned in this book.

Figure 2 is a diagram of one neurone A and its connections with other neurones. The fat part of the neurone is the cell body. The long thin extension of the cell body is known as the axon; and this branches, ending in a number of terminals, shown as c, d, and e in the diagram. The terminals are closely applied to the cell bodies of other neurones, B, C, and D, or, if not to the cell bodies, to fine outgrowths of the cell bodies known as dendrites. The spaces in between the neurones are occupied by glial cells, which help support and maintain the neurones.

Just as neurones B, C, and D can receive information from neurone A, so can A be affected by terminals on its dendrites — a and a'. Although the structure and chemistry of a neurone are complicated, the function of any one neurone is exceedingly simple. It is either 'on' or 'off'. A light switch, for example, looks complicated enough in its cardboard box before we install it. There are bits of plastic, brass screws, and other screws to hold the plastic together, and yet, like the neurone, its sole function is to be either 'on' or 'off'. This

1

Epilepsy: the facts

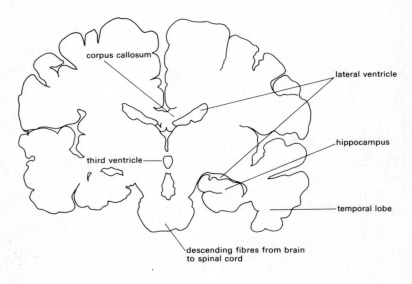

corpus callosum

lateral ventricle

hippocampus

third ventricle

temporal lobe

descending fibres from brain
to spinal cord

Fig. 1. (a) Cross-section of the brain.

concept is also the basic principle of a computer. Vast mathematical problems can be solved through the programming of
electronic switches having only the function of being 'on' or
'off'.

How does neurone A influence those with which it is in
contact? Through chemical processes, it maintains a voltage
charge across its cell membrane, like a small battery. When it
switches 'on', a wave of change in voltage sweeps through the
cell body, and down the axon to the terminals b, c, and d.
There is no direct electrical contact with the next cell. The
voltage charge in each terminal is associated with the discharge of a small quantity of a chemical known as a transmitter. The composition of the transmitter varies from one
part of the brain to another, but each neurone discharges

2

What is epilepsy?

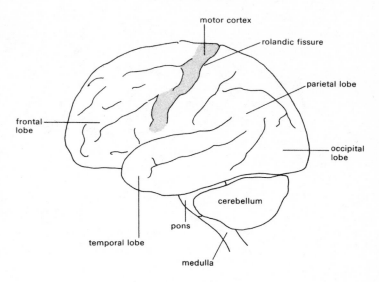

Fig. 1. (b) Side-view of the brain.

the same transmitter at each of its terminals. This transmitter diffuses across the very narrow space between the terminal and the dendrite of the next cell, and causes a voltage charge, which, if sufficient, will switch on the next cell. Cell A, for example, might switch on if terminals a and a' were activated simultaneously, but not in response to either alone.

There are also inhibitory terminals, shown in black in the diagram, which, if activated, change the voltage in the opposite direction so that cell A is *less* likely to be switched on. If these black terminals are activated they may well over-ride the joint excitatory effects of a and a'. It can be seen immediately that the probability of discharge of neurone A is influenced by the sum of excitatory and inhibitory actions of all those neurones sending terminals to it — and these may number 50 000. There is obviously considerable scope for things to go wrong!

3

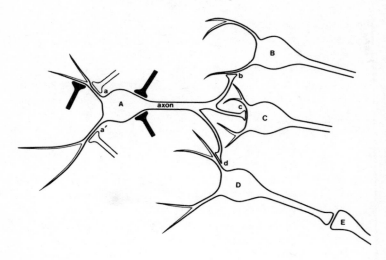

Fig. 2. Diagram of connections between nerve cells.

The events leading to a seizure

One of the ways in which events can go wrong is when a neurone loses some of the terminals coming to it because of damage to the cells of origin of these terminals. If inhibitory terminals are lost, then the cell will become hyperexcitable, and begin to switch on, or fire, inappropriately. Repetitive inappropriate firing of A may therefore kindle firing of B, C, and D, and through D yet another neurone E, and so on. More and more neurones may be incorporated into the abnormal pattern of discharge.

This is the biological background to an epileptic seizure, a paroxysmal discharge of neurones in the cerebral hemispheres. The normal, quiet function of neurones is interrupted as they are forced through their contacts into an abnormal pattern of discharge. It follows that the individual may perceive some sort of disturbance. Different types of seizure are a reflection of different patterns of paroxysmal discharge. Seizure types are described in Chapter 2 and two examples will suffice here. If the discharging neurones are in the temporal lobe of the brain, amongst those concerned with memory, the paroxysmal discharge may result in a distortion of memory so that the sufferer perceives that he has experienced ongoing events before — the phenomenon of *déjà vu*. If the seizure discharge spreads throughout large areas of the brain, then consciousness may be lost.

The electrical events described can, if occurring in sufficient numbers of neurones, be recorded by small electrodes on the surface of the scalp, amplified, and displayed on a moving strip of paper as the electroencephalogram (EEG). The use of this procedure is described in Chapter 4. In someone with established epilepsy, the EEG between seizures may well also show abnormal discharges which are not apparent to the doctor in terms of observed behaviour, nor are they associated with any change perceived by the person with epilepsy. Although the abnormal discharges on the EEG are clearly a fragment, as it were, of a seizure, they are not usually regarded as seizures. Our definition of an epileptic seizure, therefore, is *a paroxysmal discharge of cerebral neurones apparent to the subject and/or an observer.*

Terminology

It is worth making two further points about Figure 2. It is theoretically possible to protect neurones B, C, and D from the abnormal neurone A, either by using drugs which interfere with the transmitter mechanisms, or by altering the battery-like properties of the cell membrane of neurones B, C, and D. Drugs used for the treatment of epilepsy are of these types.

The second point is that abnormal firing of nerve cells does not depend solely upon structural damage to groups of nerve cells. This example was chosen solely for illustration. Anything which increases the excitability of a group of nerve cells — or which decreases the amount of inhibition, which comes to the same thing — may cause a paroxysmal neuronal discharge. For example certain gases, developed for use in war, will cause seizures of this type amongst the enemy.

Although we hope that such gases will never be used, I have deliberately introduced the topic at this point to explain the difference between the diagnosis of 'a seizure' and the diagnosis of 'epilepsy'. It would clearly be ridiculous to label as 'epileptics' those soldiers who had convulsed on exposure to the nerve gas. The cause of their seizures is readily apparent, and, not only that, the tendency to convulse is present only in the presence of the nerve gas. Someone is said to suffer from epilepsy if he has a *continuing tendency to epileptic seizures.*

This example polarizes, as it were, the explanation, but there are many grey areas, some of which I attempt to explain here, and others will become apparent elsewhere in this book. Take for example the case of a young woman who has a single seizure at the age of 19, after a rather-too-good office party at Christmas time. It would be justifiable to assume that alcohol played some part in the genesis of the seizure — but there were others who drank just as much who did not have a seizure. So we must presume that our patient has a lower *convulsive threshold* than her colleagues (see page 31). A single seizure is not considered sufficient to make the diagnosis of epilepsy, as, until time has passed, it is obviously not apparent whether this seizure will prove to be the first of others. In fact, as is discussed further in Chapter 5, about two-thirds of all such people will have a second seizure within three years.

A consultant neurologist will make a diagnosis of epilepsy when he hears of *more than one non-febrile seizure of any type. Febrile* convulsions are discussed in Chapter 8. Clearly he has no difficulty in doing this if the time scale is short, but what does he call a man who has one fit at the age of 19 and another at the age of 75? It would seem a bit nonsensical to tell the old man that he had been an epileptic all his life, as he would be obliged to do if he followed rigidly the definition of 'more than one non-febrile seizure'. Furthermore this definition, by definition, precludes epilepsy stopping. What do we call a man aged 40, who had ten seizures between the ages of 15 and 25? We cannot, unfortunately, say a cured epileptic, as he is still slightly at risk from further seizures. These examples clearly show that the label 'epilepsy' has to be applied with common sense. It is not one of those tidy diseases such as poliomyelitis, in which there is little argument about the paralysis or the viral agent causing it.

These medical uncertainties are reflected in patients' minds. After all, if a doctor cannot give a coherent definition of a disease, how can the patient be expected to understand it? The uncertainties are compounded by admixture with a series of half truths that, perhaps because epilepsy is so common, are held in the collective imagination as folk-lore — that epilepsy is inherited, that it always begins in childhood, that it is always convulsive in nature, and that it is related in some ways to mental illness. Glimpses of this stereotype of epilepsy are seen in the clinic when a patient, or his relative, says 'It can't be epilepsy because . . .'. I hope this book will dispel some of these confusions.

Part of the difficulty in understanding about epilepsy is a hangover from the ideas of the great physicians of the last century. 'Diseases' were described, for example Addison's disease, Bright's disease, and Graves's disease. Each of these has proved unexpectedly more and more complex with further research. For example Bright described the dilute urine containing protein, and the hypertension that are merely symptoms common to a number of processes resulting in chronic kidney failure. Even the 'tidy' disease — poliomyelitis — referred to above, is not really encapsulated in a neat bundle of facts. Many children are infected with the virus and escape paralysis, and we have little idea why.

With these comments in mind, the reader will find it helpful to think of an epileptic seizure as a symptom — an event that is just one of the few ways that the brain has of reacting to untoward internal processes. The continuation of such reactions constitutes epilepsy. It is the doctor's task to disentangle, if at all possible, the factors in the equation that result in seizures.

I have had some difficulty in deciding what to call the person with epilepsy throughout this book. There are some who instinctively dislike the word − or label − 'epileptic'. It is of course an adjective, and one does not talk about those with heart disease or multiple sclerosis as 'cardiacs' or 'multiple sclerotics'. I have to admit, however, that those with diabetes seem quite happy to be known as 'diabetics'. The British Epilepsy Association is keen that we should talk about a 'person with epilepsy'. I have always found the word person too *im*personal, but to write and read 'a man, woman, or child with epilepsy' takes too long, and to write each time 'those with epilepsy' seems archaic. I have avoided the use of the word patient, except in a medical context, as people with epilepsy should only become patients for brief moments in their lives. I have therefore used whatever phrase seemed most appropriate in the context, without prejudice.

What about the words used to describe epileptic seizures? The word 'seizure' is that most commonly used by neurologists for all types, but, depending upon the manifestation of the seizure, he may call them convulsions. Often he will use the words employed by his patient − for example, fit, turn, attack, or dizzy spell. If the person has two types of seizure, he often calls them 'big ones' and 'little ones', and, as long as he and the doctor find themselves talking about the same events, this is perfectly acceptable.

The word seizure is really too sudden and violent a word to describe the minor distortions of consciousness that may be the only manifestation of temporal lobe epilepsy, but we do not have a better word to cover all types. I use it throughout this book, with the exception of the section on febrile convulsions, a term hallowed by long usage, and, in any event, only distantly related to epilepsy. Strictly speaking,

8

there are other types of seizure. The World Health Organization's *Dictionary of Epilepsy* indicates that any sudden attack of cerebral origin may be called a seizure. A stroke certainly used to be called an apoplectic seizure, but by common usage in this country, seizure now means an epileptic event.

Sometimes in correspondence and conversation doctors employ the words 'epileptiform' or 'epileptoid'. In my experience, doctors who use such terms are skating round the subject and avoiding frankly stating that their patient has had an epileptic seizure. The only justification for such a term might be the description of attacks which are due to a clearly defined and reversible cause — for example by an inadequate supply of oxygen to the brain, as might occur by mischance during an anaesthetic. Even then it would be preferable, in my view, to call the episode an 'anoxic seizure' rather than an 'epileptiform seizure due to anoxia'.

How common is epilepsy?

In spite of the difficulties of definition described above, some attempt must be made to assess the frequency of epilepsy. First, I explain two terms. The *incidence* of a disorder is the number of new cases occurring in a defined group of people in a defined period of time — for example x new cases per 100 000 per year. The group may be further defined by race, sex, or age, but, unless otherwise stated, the group is assumed to be representative of the population as a whole.

The *prevalence* of a disease is the number of cases in a group of people at any one defined time. For example the incidence of the common cold in the United Kingdom is very high, perhaps 60 000 per 100 000 per year, but the prevalence of those *suffering symptoms on any one day* as assessed by a special survey might be *2 000 per 100 000*.

Accurate figures for the incidence of new cases of epilepsy, as defined by the occurrence of more than one non-febrile seizure, come from the population of Olmstead County in

9

Epilepsy: the facts

Minnesota. The population of this rural part of the United States has the good fortune to be cared for by doctors at the Mayo Clinic. Research workers there, led by Professor Kurland, have long had an interest in identifying all patients with epilepsy. Figure 3 shows a graph of the incidence of

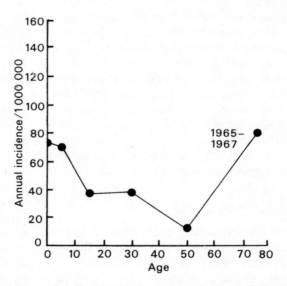

Fig. 3. Incidence of epilepsy at various ages. (Redrawn with permission from Hauser and Kurland, *Epilepsia* (1975).)

epilepsy plotted against age. It can be seen that the incidence of new cases is highest in infancy and in old age, but new cases can occur at any age. The average annual incidence rate over a period of more than 30 years was found to be 49 per 100 000 per year. If one considers the average life span as 70 years it can immediately be calculated that in one life one has a (49 × 70 × 100)/100 000 per cent chance of developing epilepsy. This sum works out as the surprisingly high figure of 3.4 per cent and immediately explains the potential demand for this book!

10

What is epilepsy?

Epilepsy is thus not a rare or unusual disorder, but one which impinges upon the lives of many of us. If the incidence rate for single seizures that remain isolated is combined with the incidence rate for recurring epileptic seizures, it can be calculated that about 5.9 per cent of the total population of the community may be expected to have one or more afebrile (see p. 6) seizures at some stage of their lives. There are no reasons to suppose that the United Kingdom population is significantly different from the United States population in this respect.

The frequency of continuing seizures in the population is judged by the prevalence — and here we again run into difficulties of definition. Clearly common sense dictates that if someone had a seizure the day before our survey day, they should be included, but what about someone who had many seizures in the past, but none for three years? One has to judge where to draw the line. In my survey, with Graham Scambler, of those over the age of 16 with epilepsy in the community on the registration lists of seventeen general practitioners in Metropolitan London, I included all those with more than one non-febrile seizure of any type with at least one seizure in the two years preceding the survey date. The prevalence figure for active epilepsy, as so defined, was found to be 235/100 000 adults. Virtually all these were on anti-epileptic drugs.

There was also a group of adults (110/100 000) who were still on anticonvulsants, although they had not had a seizure of any type for more than two years. It may be assumed that their general practitioners thought a return of seizures was likely if the drugs were omitted.

A similar survey was carried out by Professor Rutter and his colleagues amongst children on the Isle of Wight. He found that 730 out of 100 000 children between the ages of 5 and 14 were on anticonvulsant drugs, and 430 out of 100 000 had had a seizure within the last one year.

If we translate the experience of these surveys to that of a typical English general practitioner, he will have registered

11

under his care about four adults and three or four children who have had a fit in the last two years, and about two adults and two children who remain on anticonvulsants for seizures in the past.

In United Kingdom national terms, such calculations show that there are about 136 000 adults and 90 000 children on anticonvulsants, of whom about 94 000 adults and 54 000 children have active epilepsy, as judged by seizures within the last one or two years. To these figures must be added the numbers in long-stay accommodation and special centres for epilepsy. The problems of these unfortunates, suffering the very worse epilepsy usually in association with some other disorder dating from birth, are discussed on pages 141–2.

2

The different types of epileptic seizure

Figure 4 illustrates the two main classes of origin of seizure. In the top third of the figure, the hatched area indicates a number of neurones which are in some way abnormal, having a tendency to discharge paroxysmally. They can, as explained in the last chapter, drive other neurones to follow their abnormal patterns of discharge. The paths of influence of the discharging neurones are indicated by the arrows. As long as the discharge remains in one part of the brain, the seizure is said to be a *partial seizure*. What happens during a partial seizure depends upon the exact site and pattern of discharge of abnormal neurones. Temporal lobe seizures are of this type. The clinically observed features of these and other types of partial seizures are described on pp. 17–21.

The abnormal discharge may spread through the connections linking the two halves of the brain, or, by affecting poorly identified central collections of cells, initiate a generalized seizure discharge, in which case the seizure is said to be a *partial seizure with secondary generalization* (to grand mal). This is shown in the middle third of Figure 4.

The lower third of Figure 4 illustrates the second main class of seizure. In this, central collections of cells are themselves in some way abnormal in their behaviour – even though they may seem structually perfectly normal under the microscope. Because of their central position, and the direction and power of their transmissions, a seizure discharge generated within them spreads more or less simultaneously to all parts of the brain. Such a seizure, generalized at onset, is a *primary generalized seizure*. Petit mal absence seizures, and some grand mal seizures, are of this type.

13

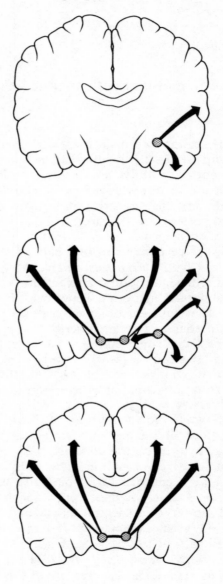

The different types of epileptic seizure

Grand mal seizures (generalized convulsion)

Whether the paroxysmal discharge be primary, or secondarily generalized from a focus in the cortex (the name given to the layers of neurones on the surface of the brain) consciousness is lost.

Cerebral neurones are connected to other neurones in the spinal cord. The axons of some of these pass through nerves to innervate muscles. The powerful generalized cortical seizure discharge is therefore linked through this direct transmission system to muscle fibres. Disordered contraction of all muscles is the hallmark of a grand mal seizure.

The first phase of a grand mal seizure is known as the tonic (contraction) phase. At this stage, because of widespread contraction of muscles, the body is rigid, and incapable of maintaining a normal co-ordinated posture so that the subject falls to the ground. The respiratory muscles also contract, forcing the air in the chest out through the larynx, so there may be an involuntary noise — a grunt or a cry — at the onset of the attack. The jaw muscles also contract, and, because the normal associated movements that keep the tongue out of the way are disordered by the seizure discharge, the tongue or cheek may be bitten.

During the tonic phase there are no co-ordinated movements of breathing, yet muscular contraction caused by the seizure discharge is vigorous. This combination of events means that the oxygen supply in the blood is rapidly depleted, and the subject will become a dusky blue colour, the technical name for which is cyanosis. This colour is exaggerated by suffusion of blood vessels in the face and eyes by

Fig. 4. Different types of epileptic seizure.
Top: Partial seizure — the paroxysmal discharge spreads locally from a focus of abnormal cells.
Middle: Partial seizure with secondary generalization — the discharge spreads locally, and also to brainstem structures which spread the discharge widely through the brain.
Bottom: Primary generalized seizure — the discharge spreads symmetrically throughout the brain from the beginning.

15

raised pressure within the thorax, due to the strong contraction of chest muscles. Normal movements of swallowing are lost, so that saliva often dribbles out between the tightly clenched teeth, although I have never seen the so called 'frothing at the mouth' and doubt that it exists. The disordered contraction of abdominal and bladder muscles may result in incontinence of urine, though this is by no means invariable. Dilatation of the pupils and sweating often occur.

After one or two minutes of the tonic phase, the seizure passes into the clonic or convulsive phase, with rhythmic movements of limbs and trunk muscles. These gradually cease after a few minutes, and the subject lies passively unconscious, often breathing stertorously. Normal colour returns. Consciousness gradually lightens, so that the subject can be roused; he begins to move around, and then he can be helped to his feet and a chair. For several minutes after this, he will be confused and restless. After this he may suffer a headache for the rest of the day, or go to bed and sleep for a couple of hours. He will also be aware of stiff and painful muscles which have contracted forcibly during the seizure.

Petit mal seizures (typical absence).

Although a translation of petit mal is the 'little illness', petit mal is not synonymous with 'minor epilepsy' as there are all sorts of small attacks which are *not* attacks of petit mal. True petit mal seizures, or typical absences are, by modern definition, associated with a characteristic electro-encephalographic discharge, which is illustrated on page 73. Short-lived partial seizures arising from a focus of abnormal neurones in one temporal lobe of the brain (see page 19) may be very similar on clinical grounds, but the distinction is worth making because of the difference in cause, treatment and outcome between the two types of seizure.

Petit mal is virtually invariably a disorder of childhood. A typical attack is very brief, lasting only a few seconds. The onset and termination are abrupt. The child will suddenly cease what he is doing, stare, look a little pale, perhaps flutter his eyelids, and drop his head slightly forwards. Posture of the limbs and trunk is usually maintained so the child does not fall. After the seizure the child resumes what he has been doing. Because the interruption of the normal stream of consciousness is so brief, attacks may be unobserved by parents, and not remarked upon by the affected children. I have seen a typical attack in a supermarket. A girl aged about nine was helping her mother unload a wire basket at the checkout. She suddenly paused with a pot of honey held in the air between basket and counter, fluttered her eyelids, and then continued transferring the purchases without further pause.

Whereas one would be unfortunate to have more than one grand mal seizure in a day, petit mal seizures may be very frequent — 10 to 50 seizures a day being occasionally encountered. Fortunately most children only have occasional attacks.

Petit mal is often associated with *myoclonic jerks,* which are particularly frequent soon after waking. These are brief shock-like contractions of the muscles, which are so short-lived it is meaningless to ask whether consciousness is disturbed or not. I have heard this described as 'the flying saucer syndrome' in reference to the broken crockery that may occur at breakfast-time!

Partial seizures (focal seizures).

The exact internal perception or external manifestations of partial seizures depend upon the site of origin of discharge of abnormal neurones. If these lie in the part of the brain called the motor cortex, a strip of brain concerned with movement (Figure 5; see also Figure 1(b), p. 3), the initial manifestation will be a contraction of muscles in the opposite side of the body. (The axons of cerebral neurones in the motor strip cross to the opposite side of the body in the part of the brain just above the spinal cord, known as the medulla oblongata.)

The threshold of excitation of cells in the motor strip

17

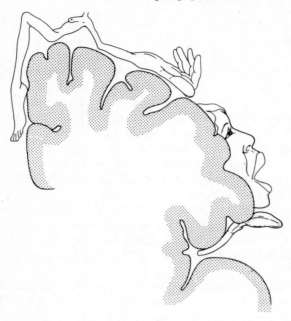

Fig. 5. Motor cortex of human brain. Electrical stimulation of the shaded area of cortex causes movement of the opposite part of the body, indicated by the representation of the human figure. Note the large area of cortex dedicated to movements of the fingers, lips, and tongue.

seems to be lowest for cells which supply the index finger and thumb, the corner of the mouth, or the big toe. Not only are the thresholds of excitation lowest, but there are more cells assigned to controlling these muscles, which are concerned with the fine tuning of manual skills and facial expression. Statistically, therefore, there is a greater chance of abnormal events occurring in these cells. The first evidence of such a seizure may thus be twitching at one corner of the mouth. As the seizure discharge spreads, the muscles around the eyes are next involved, as cerebral neurones supplying these muscles are contiguous to those supplying the mouth. Next involved are the hand muscles, and next the foot

18

muscles. This march of events was described in the last century independently by Bravais, a French neurologist, and by Hughlings Jackson, an English neurologist whose wife had such attacks. This type of seizure is often called a *Jacksonian seizure*. It may occur with no disturbance of consciousness whatsoever, although, in common with other partial seizures, secondary generalization with loss of consciousness can occur.

Another type of partial seizure with movement is known as a *versive seizure*. In this the head and eyes turn to one side. Usually the arm to which they are turned is elevated and twitches. Sometimes the 'version' may continue so that the subject turns round several times on his own axis. Version is usually in the direction away from the discharging cerebral neurones — a left hemisphere focus causes turning to the right. Such seizures are therefore called *adversive*.

In the types of seizure described so far, there is an external manifestation — contraction of muscles driven by the discharging cerebral neurones. The subject is aware of the twitching, so that this seizure is easily apparent to both subject and observer.

Other groups of discharging cerebral neurones may not necessarily result in any external apparent event, only in a distorted internal perception. A focus in one parietal lobe (see Figure 1) may only result in a transient disturbance of sensation, such as a perception of pins and needles, in the opposite side of the face, arm, or leg. A seizure discharge in the anterior part of the temporal lobe may result only in the subject perceiving a strange smell, unreal, often unpleasant, and yet often vaguely familiar. Similar hallucinations of distorted taste may also occur, which are usually perceived as unpleasant.

If the seizure discharge begins in a slightly different part of the temporal lobe, complex visual hallucinations may occur. One boy of 11 told me that he saw himself standing near a shower with another boy, whom he felt he knew yet could not name. This boy and he alternately put their feet

19

under the running water, and this bizarre hallucination continued until the seizure ended.

Other seizures arising in the temporal lobe may cause a perception that events taking place have previously occurred in the subject's experience. This phenomenon is known as '*déjà vu*'. *Jamais vu* is a phrase used to indicate that the subject perceives familiar surroundings as unreal.

If such distorted perceptions occur, it is clear that full consciousness — as defined by awareness of current events, interpretation of current events, and correct responsiveness to current events — is not maintained. All gradations of disturbance may be seen. For example the subject may respond appropriately to a question after a considerable delay, or he may respond inappropriately, or not at all. After the attack has terminated, he may say that he was dimly aware of ongoing real events, but this is not necessarily true, and the subject may be amnesic for all events during and for some time after the seizure.

Arrest of speech without significant disturbance of consciouness may be due to a seizure discharge occurring in the anterior part of the temporal lobe of the so called dominant hemisphere, which is nearly always on the left side, in association with preferred right handedness. Such a seizure is called an *aphasic partial seizure.*

Sometimes seizures arising in the temporal lobe result in complex automatic behaviour — the so-called *psychomotor seizure.* The subject may, for example, dress and undress repeatedly or drum his fingers on the table. Less complex, but more common manifestations, are repeated sucking or chewing or swallowing movements. The subject will have no memory for these events after the attack.

Such automatic behaviour occurring during the seizure discharge must be distinguished from the very common confusion following a grand mal attack, or following a prolonged temporal lobe seizure, for which the subject will also be amnesic. This amnesia is, perhaps, analogous to the amnesia following a head injury, in which, for example, a man will

20

competently complete a game of rugby football after a collision resulting in a concussive head injury, yet afterwards he will be amnesic for this part of the game.

Emotional experiences are very frequent in partial seizures arising in the temporal lobe. These are often expressed just as 'a horrible feeling', but sometimes the sensation of fear is overpowering.

Sensations in the abdomen and chest often also occur. A common initial sensation is a vague feeling of discomfort in the upper abdomen, which rises rapidly into the chest and head. The abdominal sensation may be accompanied by contractions of the stomach and bowel resulting in audible rumbles.

Another frequent internal sensation is one of vertigo. Very often people with seizures beginning in the temporal lobe say that they are 'dizzy'. This word is used in different senses by different people, but a minority appear to perceive true, or rotational, vertigo as part of the seizure.

Rarer types of seizure

Atypical absences (petit mal variant).

This phrase is used in two different ways — to describe absences which are clinically similar to typical absences which are associated with atypical EEG records, and to describe absences in association with other features, of which loss of postural control is the most marked. In these so called 'akinetic drop attacks' the child may crash to the floor with such force and frequency that he has to wear a crash helmet to protect his head from damage.

Clonic seizures.

The distinction between these and myoclonic jerks (page 17) is slight. If jerks are multiple, then the seizures tend to be called clonic.

21

Epilepsy: the facts

Tonic seizures

A tonic (rigid) posturing of all limbs without a clonic phase is sometimes seen in some generalized cerebral disorders in childhood. Unfortunately the same name is given to one rare form of partial seizure in which one part of the body briefly adopts a tonic posture.

Infantile spasms (*salaam seizures; West's syndrome*)

These seizures of infancy are characterized by a brief, sudden flexion of head, trunk, and limbs, as if the baby is bowing a 'salaam'.

The relation between types of seizure and types of epilepsy

Figure 6 shows three interlocking circles, the area of which is roughly proportional to the frequency of occurrence of various types of seizure. The central one incorporates the set of grand mal seizures. The left-hand circle contains the set of partial siezures, many of which become secondarily generalized, as indicated by the considerable overlap between these two sets. In so far as we believe that all partial seizures arise from some focal area of structural abnormality within the brain, all partial seizures, and those seizures which are secondarily generalized from some focal onset, can be said to be symptomatic of some underlying problem — so-called *symptomatic epilepsy*.

The right-hand circle indicates typical absences (petit mal seizures). About 30 per cent of children with petit mal also have grand mal seizures, as is indicated by the overlap between right hand and centre circles. Such primary generalized epilepsy is *never* symptomatic of underlying structural brain disease, and may be said to be constitutional or *idiopathic epilepsy*.

The area of the centre circle that is not overlapped by the left and right hand circles is the set of those subjects who

22

The different types of epileptic seizure

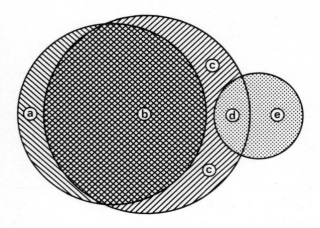

Fig. 6. Relation between different types of epileptic seizure and different types of epilepsy. a = partial seizures alone; b = partial seizures evolving to tonic–clonic seizures; c = tonic–clonic seizures of uncertain origin; d = tonic–clonic seizures in association with typical absences; e = typical absences alone. a + b = symptomatic epilepsy. c = cryptogenic epilepsy. d + e = idiopathic epilepsy (primary generalized or constitutional epilepsy).

only have grand mal epilepsy. Such *cryptogenic epilepsy* (epilepsy of hidden cause), less common since the advent of sophisticated investigations, should not be called idiopathic. Two possibilities exist – either the petit mal trait was not overt in childhood, and grand mal seizures are the only manifestation of idiopathic epilepsy, or the seizure discharge from a small lesion becomes generalized so quickly that its initial partial phase is overlooked. Very often, it is difficult to distinguish between the two possibilities even with prolonged EEG recording.

The frequency with which different types of seizure occur

This depends very much upon the group of epileptics studied. Table 1 shows the prevalence of different types of seizure in those with epilepsy in the community in the survey described

Table 1. *Types of seizure and recent activity: percentage of those with epilepsy over the age 16 in community survey in London.*

	Petit mal	Partial seizures	Grand mal	Seizure of any type
Experienced in last six months	2	34	26	50
Experienced in last two years	2	45	47	69
Ever experienced	7	56	95	100

on page 43. For the purposes of this Table those who were still on anticonvulsants for seizures in the past are grouped with those who have had more than one non-febrile seizure, with at least one seizure in the last two years. Note the high proportion — 56 per cent — who have had partial seizures at some time. In a further 12 per cent, even though overt partial seizures had not occurred, there was clear clinical evidence of focal onset to the generalized attacks (see the discussion on auras on page 25), or EEG evidence of focal onset to the generalized attacks. Thus in 68 per cent of the sample, regardless of any history indicating structural damage to the brain, there was evidence of a focal, and therefore presumably structural, origin for the seizures. The experience of neurologists since that survey indicates that more vigorous exploration with more advanced EEG recording techniques and new radiological techniques (see page 76) would increase that proportion even further. Idiopathic epilepsy, in adults at least, is not common.

The proportions of different types of seizure in childhood were documented in Professor Rutter's Isle of Wight survey. Seventy-seven per cent had had a grand mal seizure, 37 per cent partial seizures, 12 per cent petit mal seizures, 6 per cent myclonic seizures, and 2 per cent had had 'salaam' fits. Of those who had had grand mal seizures, only 33 per cent had had an attack in the previous year.

The different types of epileptic seizure

Further definitions

Before discussing the causes of epilepsy in the next chapter, there are a few more aspects of epileptic seizures that require explanation.

Some subjects may have a warning of an impending seizure. The first type of warning is a vague feeling of an impending seizure, particularly before grand mal seizures. This *prodrome* may last several hours. It has no obvious physiological explanation, but it is remarked upon too often by subjects to be lightly dismissed as due to imaginary reconstruction of events. The prodrome is usually unpleasant — a feeling of mental heaviness or depression. Less commonly, elation and energetic activity may herald a seizure. The second type of warning, known as an *aura*, is not really a warning at all, but the initial symptom of the seizure itself. Examples of such auras include the epigastric sensation of partial seizures arising in one part of the temporal lobe (page 21), or the brief tingling in one hand which precedes a partial seizure arising in the parietal lobe which rapidly generalizes to a grand mal seizure.

Another phrase requiring definition is *post-ictal paresis*. An *ictus* is another synonym for a seizure. Post-ictal paresis indicates weakness of left or right limbs following a convulsion affecting primarily those limbs. Sometimes known as Todd's paresis, after the neurologist who first described it, it invariably indicates structural damage in the hemisphere on the side opposite to the weak limbs. The weakness may last from a few minutes up to 48 hours. Post-ictal amnesia, post-ictal confusion, post-ictal sleep, and post-ictal headache have already been described. *Post-ictal automatism* is the phenomenon in which a person can undertake some fairly complex act, such as undressing and putting themselves to bed, of which they have no subsequent memory.

Status epilepticus is a phrase used to indicate seizures occurring so close together that one seizure runs into another, without recovery of normal cerebral function between seizures. This may happen with any type of seizure, so that a neurologist speaks of petit mal status, temporal lobe status, or grand mal status. In the first two types, the diagnosis may be difficult to reach unless the subject is already known to the neurologist. The patient may be found in the street or at home confused and inaccessible to conversation because of continuing seizure discharges.

Grand mal status epilepticus, in which the subject does not recover consciousness between generalized tonic–clonic convulsions, is a medical emergency. The lack of normal respiratory movements, in association with the extreme muscular contractions during the seizures, throw a considerable stress upon the cardiovascular system. The principles of treatment of this serious but fortunately uncommon state are discussed on pages 102–3, but early admission to hospital is essential.

Finally, a partial seizure in which the seizure discharge continues but remains confined to one part of the pre-Rolandic motor cortex (Figures 1(b) and 5) results in continuous twitching of muscles in one part of a limb on the opposite side of the body. For example the index finger and thumb may continue to twitch for days or even weeks, without any spread of seizure discharge to other muscles, and with no disturbance of consciousness. This is known as *epilepsia partialis continua.*

3

The causes of epilepsy

One aspect of human nature and intelligence is to search for causal links between events. The onset of epileptic seizures in an infant, or previously healthy child or adult, results in great heart-searching in the family, and raking over past events in an attempt to find some reason. Yet it has to be admitted that the most careful medical assessment of past events or current state allows a neurologist to assign a cause or causes of epilepsy in only a minority of subjects, and then often on the basis of circumstantial evidence.

Take head injury, for example. If a child is known to have cut his head in the playground, and then has his first seizure two weeks later, many parents will link the two events, and attribute the onset of epilepsy to this minor head injury on no basis other than coincidence in time. The same sequence of events − a minor cranial accident − affecting an adult industrial worker may unfortunately lead to litigation between employer and employee, as the latter holds that he 'was perfectly all right before the accident'. The association of events in time is no evidence of cause. It is however perfectly true that severe head injuries may result in the development of epilepsy, so-called post-traumatic epilepsy, as is discussed on page 35. Somewhere, therefore, in the continuum of mild to moderate to severe head injuries there must be a zone where there is reasonable doubt as to whether epilepsy was or was not caused by the injury.

The same arguments apply when assessing the effects of a difficult birth and the possible relationship of that to the subsequent development of epilepsy. There is no doubt that a very difficult labour, especially if the baby is small, may cause significant brain damage. Mental retardation, cerebral palsy, and epilepsy may result. However, after many difficult or prolonged labours the child develops perfectly normally. It used to be thought that forceps or breech deliveries might be blamed for the subsequent development of epilepsy. However a study of all children born in one week in 1958 in England, Scotland, and Wales showed that epilepsy was no more likely to develop after such births than after normal unassisted deliveries.

Having given these warnings against uncritically linking life events and the development of epilepsy, what are the factors which can be said, with a fair degree of confidence, to cause epilepsy? The causes are different at different ages. Table 2 illustrates this. Some causes, such as severe birth injury, cause seizures in the neonatal period, and the scarred brain may cause seizures throughout life, as is indicated by the long continuing arrow in the Table. Other causes occur only at one age, and their effect then ceases. Metabolic disturbances in the neonatal period, such as hypoglycaemia, are examples of this. Each main group of causes is now explained in detail.

Inheritance

Until about 30 years ago most doctors believed that inheritance was a major factor in causing epilepsy. This belief is still strong amongst the population at large. I am often told: 'It can't be epilepsy because there is nothing like that in the family'. These views were held with such force in some states of America and in some Scandinavian countries that it was illegal for epileptics to marry. It is certainly true that genetic factors do play a part in epilepsy, but not an overwhelming part.

Inheritance of epilepsy can occur in a number of different ways. The first is the most definite, but the most unusual. There are some genetic diseases in which the gene is *recessive*. That is to say the effects of the gene will only be expressed if a child has a double dose of the relevant gene — one gene

28

The causes of epilepsy

Table 2. *Causes of epilepsy at different ages*

Cause	Newborn	Infant	Child	Adult
Genetic		Lipidoses, Tuberose sclerosis	'Idiopathic', Neurofibromatosis	'Idiopathic', Tuberose sclerosis, Neurofibromatosis
Congenital			Angioma	Angioma
Anoxia*	At birth	Febrile convulsions		
Trauma	At birth		Head injury, Intracranial surgery	Head injury, Intercranial surgery
Tumours			Tumours	Tumours
Infectious diseases (bacteria, viruses, parasites)	Meningitis	Meningitis, Encephalitis	Meningitis, Encephalitis, Abscess	Meningitis, Encephalitis, Abscess
Acquired metabolic disease	Hypoglycaemia, Hypercalcaemia			Chronic renal failure
Alcohol				Chronic alcohol abuse
Degenerative disorders				Dementia

* Reduction of oxygen supply to the brain

29

from each parent. The parents, although themselves carrying the gene, do not show the abnormality as the other member of their pair of genes is normal. They are said to be symptom-less carriers. There are certain rare disorders of metabolism of the brain collectively known as the lipidoses, which are inherited by recessive genes. Lipids are important constituents of the membranes surrounding the cell bodies, axons, and dendrites of the neurone. A disorder of the structure and function of the cell membrane may well lead to paroxysmal discharge of neurones − an epileptic seizure. Examples of such lipidoses causing epilepsy include Gaucher's disease and Tay–Sachs disease.

In other genetically determined diseases, inheritance is through a dominant gene. One of the parents carrying the gene will therefore not only show the effects of the gene him-self or herself, but will transmit the effective gene to, on average, half his or her children, the other children receiving the other member of the relevant gene pair. Tuberose sclerosis and neurofibromatosis, disorders of glial cells (page 1), are transmitted in this way.

It must be stressed that these diseases are rare. They have been mentioned first only because the mechanism of their inheritance is most clearly understood.

There is, however, also good evidence that primary gener-alized idiopathic epilepsy, as defined on page 22 is also inherited. In order to explain this it is easier to argue back from a child with epilepsy to his parents, rather than first considering the chances of a prospective parent with epilepsy having an epileptic child, a problem which is considered on page 33. The characteristic EEG (Fig. 10) is seen in about 40 per cent of brothers and sisters of children with primary generalized epilepsy, even if these brothers and sisters have not had any overt seizures. That is to say, the biochemical ab-normality which causes the abnormal EEG record is inherited, but this abnormality is not necessarily expressed in clinically apparent seizures. A smaller proportion of the parents of children with primary generalized epilepsy will also show the

The causes of epilepsy

characteristic EEG changes. We know from following children with these changes that the characteristic discharges become much less frequent with age, so the absence of discharges in adult life does not mean that the parent did not have unrecorded and unapparent discharges in childhood. From mathematical studies of the records of many families with primary generalized epilepsy, it has been calculated that the responsible biochemical abnormality is transmitted as a dominant gene from one parent to half the children of any marriage in which one parent carries the responsible gene. For the child to show an abnormality in cases of dominant inheritance, only one member of the pair of relevant genes needs to be abnormal. However, other gene pairs may to some extent succeed in suppressing this gene from expressing itself in overt seizures. Only about one-third of the children to whom it is transmitted will have seizures, and therefore one-sixth (the product of one-half and one-third) of all the children of the marriage. Furthermore, even if the gene is expressed in seizures, the result may only be a few petit mal seizures in childhood.

The variability in clinical expression of the inherited biochemical abnormality accounts for the occurrence of primary generalized epilepsy in a child of parents neither of whom has ever had an overt seizure. In this case one assumes that one parent does indeed have the gene, and, had an EEG been recorded in his or her childhood, one would have seen the typical EEG discharge.

Another aspect is the inheritance of a *convulsive threshold*. As explained on page 6, any one of us can be made to have a seizure if the stimulus is strong enough, and some of us do at lower levels of stimulus — at lower thresholds — than others. The inheritance of this level of threshold is probably polygenic — that is to say, several genes, some recessive and some dominant, interact to produce the final result. Another example of polygenic inheritance is height — tall parents tending to have tall children.

This inherited convulsive threshold is a background, as it

were, to the whole of the area in Table 2 to the right of the first column. It influences even those cases in which epilepsy clearly seems to be secondary to some obvious cause, such as a severe head injury causing local cortical scarring. Head injuries obviously are not inherited as such. Nevertheless there is a slight tendency for those who develop epilepsy after head injury to have a family history of epilepsy more often than those who do not develop epilepsy after what may be regarded as a comparable injury. What is being inherited here, through a number of different genes, is a lower-than-average convulsive threshold. The children of such head-injured parents are not likely to have seizures unless some additional cerebral damage affects them. It would be an unlucky family in which two members suffered severe head injuries, so that the risk of 'inheriting' epilepsy from a parent with epilepsy secondary to some structural brain damage is small.

There is, however, one group of subjects in whom inherited and acquired characteristics interplay in a complex way. The tendency to febrile convulsions (see pages 143–7) is inherited, possibly through a single dominant gene with incomplete expression, possibly through a number of genes (polygenic inheritance). If a child has had a febrile convulsion, the risk of a similar febrile convulsion affecting a brother or sister is as high as 25 per cent. A febrile convulsion, if prolonged, may damage one or other temporal lobes of the brain through lack of oxygen occurring during the seizure. The scar in the temporal lobe may then act as a focus from which paroxysmal neuronal discharges — seizures — spread in later childhood and adult life.

If I am asked by a young married couple, one of whom has epilepsy, what the chances are of any child of theirs having epilepsy, my first duty is to characterize the seizure type as accurately as possible, using the description of the seizures and the EEG recording. If it is clear that the prospective parent is having partial seizures, or generalized seizures which have a clear focal onset, either clinically or demonstrated on the EEG, then, as explained on page 22, these seizures must be secondary to some area of cortical scarring. The risk of any child of this marriage having epilepsy is only moderately higher than the risk of the general population of children. It is, however, somewhat higher than the risk of the general population because of the inheritance of the convulsive threshold. If it is clear that the prospective parent has primary generalized epilepsy, then I have to say that about half his or her children will be at risk from epilepsy, but only about one-sixth of his or her children will have overt seizures. Even so, the chances of epilepsy being a significant problem in the life of a child of a parent with primary generalized epilepsy is no more than of the order of five per cent.

Congenital malformation

A congenital abnormality, though present at birth, is not inherited. For example the abnormalities in the limbs of the children whose mothers had taken thalidomide during pregnancy are congenital, and will not be passed on to their children.

The commonest congenital abnormality relevant to epilepsy is a mal-development of blood vessels known as an angioma. The abnormal vessels may be either arterial, venous, or capillary. Often it is difficult to decide exactly what has gone wrong, but all angiomas shunt arterial blood too quickly through to veins, thereby starving some neighbouring neurones of oxygen, and causing a seizure focus. Sometimes a clot or thrombus forms in one or more of the abnormal vessels, exacerbating the situation.

One type of capillary angioma of the brain is associated with a similar malformation of blood vessels in the skin of the upper part of the face — the Sturge–Weber syndrome. Children with this particular combination of angiomatous abnormalities have a high probability of developing seizures.

Anoxia

This word means lack of sufficient oxygen, an essential component of the normal ongoing chemistry of the cell. Cerebral neurones are amongst the highest consumers of oxygen in the body, as reflected in the fact that a quarter of all arterial blood goes to the brain. If the oxygen supply is cut off, then damage to neurones occurs after a few minutes. Some neurones die, but others are damaged in such a way that they may paroxysmally discharge in subsequent life.

Anoxia may occur at birth. During each uterine contraction in a prolonged labour the foetal heart rate slows, and the supply of oxygenated blood to the brain is reduced. The umbilical cord may become tightly wound around the baby's neck. The placenta may separate prematurely. After birth, for a variety of reasons, the child may not breathe for a few minutes. These are four examples of how anoxic brain damage can occur at birth. If severe, the brain damage results in mental retardation, cerebral palsy, or epilepsy.

Anoxia also occurs in febrile convulsions, as has already been discussed. During a seizure the oxygen requirements of cerebral neurones are enormously increased, and yet the resulting convulsion interferes with normal respiration, so that the blood leaving the lungs picks up insufficient oxygen. The combination of excessive demand and inadequate supply results in anoxic damage to cerebral neurones. The neurones which seem most susceptible to damage, at the age at which febrile convulsions occur, are in the hippocampus in the temporal lobe (see Figure 1(a) on page 2).

A stroke is usually due to an obstruction to an arterial branch to one particular part of the brain, so that neurones in the territory supplied by the blocked vessel either die, or become damaged in such a way that they may form a focus for paroxysmal discharges later. Most strokes occur in late adult life, and cerebrovascular disease accounts for much of the epilepsy beginning in old age. Occasionally, however, strokes occur in young adults or even infants.

Trauma

Damage to cerebral neurones may occur through physical

trauma. Penetrating missiles such as shrapnel are, in war-time, a potent source of epilepsy. About 45 per cent of survivors develop later seizures. In civilian life most head injuries are closed — that is to say there is no penetration of the skull. However the impact of the head with the dashboard or road in road traffic injuries may cause the later development of post-traumatic epilepsy.

Professor Bryan Jennett of Glasgow has done a great deal to illuminate the factors in a head injury that are most likely to cause later epilepsy (Figure 8). The first is the duration of the post-traumatic amnesia (PTA). This is the name given to the period after a head injury when the patient, although conscious, is not recording in his memory on-going events, even though he may seem to be behaving rationally at the time. A typical story is for a head-injured person to have no recollection of relatives visiting him in hospital, even though he talked and joked with them. The duration of post-traumatic amnesia may vary from a few minutes, when the term 'concussion' is often loosely applied, to many weeks or

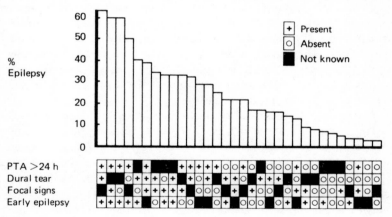

Fig. 8. Incidence of late epilepsy after compound depressed fracture of the skull in which three or four factors were known. (Redrawn from W. B. Jennett (1970). *Epilepsy after non-missile head injuries.* Heineman, London, with kind permission.)

35

even months. The mechanism of the amnesia is not known, but a useful analogy is to consider a blancmange in a mould. A vigorous tap or shaking of the mould may cause oscillations so violent within the blancmange that cracks appear within its structure, even though the mould remains intact. Such shearing forces can be demonstrated within the brains of animals subject to experimental head injuries. The longer the duration of post-traumatic amnesia, the greater the chance of the development of later epilepsy.

The second factor which Professor Jennett found to be important was the presence of focal neurological signs, such as changes in the reflexes, after the inury. Presumably these just reflect a greater degree of disruption of the cerebrum.

The third factor was the presence of local damage to the cortical surface of the brain, as judged by the presence of a tear in the dura — the membrane covering the brain. The impact of the head on a sharp corner may cause a depressed fracture, with fragments of bone tearing the dura and becoming embedded in the cortex.

Professor Jennett found that if all three factors were present in one case (a prolonged amnesia of more than 24 hours after the head injury, focal neurological signs, and a dural tear), then there was a 40 per cent chance of developing epileptic seizures later. If none of these factors was present the risk was about two per cent, about the same as that in the caseload of the general practitioner.

Professor Jennett also noted that some head-injured patients had a seizure in the first week after the injury. The occurrence of such an event — perhaps the marker of an inherited low convulsive threshold — was a potent predictor of late post-traumatic epilepsy. A seizure in the first week, accompanied by a long post-traumatic amnesia and focal neurological signs was followed by later seizures in 60 per cent of cases, even if the dura was not torn.

There are other types of head injury apart from those caused by the ubiquitous road traffic and industrial accidents.

The causes of epilepsy

The first is birth trauma. Damage to the brain at birth may be due to anoxia, as has already been discussed, but there may be direct trauma to the brain as the head is distorted in its passage down the birth canal. Precipitate labour, in which there is a sudden re-expansion of the head on delivery, may tear blood vessels within and around the brain; such damage may result in epileptic seizures in the newborn period which may continue at intervals throughout life.

Cerebral trauma also occurs, unavoidably, during cranial operations. For example small balloon-like swellings on arteries at the base of the brain are never, by themselves, responsible for epilepsy. In order to avoid the risk of haemorrhage, operation may be advised. The surgeon, in approaching the aneurysms in order to clip the neck of the 'balloons', has to handle and retract, albeit very gently, normal brain. Unfortunately seizures may follow such handling of cerebral tissues.

Tumours

A tumour arising within the brain understandably causes great anxiety — perhaps more so than with tumours elsewhere in the body, as a brain tumour may appear to strike at the very centre of one's soul and being. Many people with simple headaches due to anxiety or unhappiness believe that they have a brain tumour which is causing their headache. However the incidence of primary tumour is very low (10 per 100 000 per year). The average English general practitioner will see one new brain tumour every few years. It is however true that tumours can cause epilepsy, probably by interference with surrounding neurones.

Brain tumours are either primary or secondary. A secondary tumour is one that has been carried in the blood to the brain from another site. Cancer of the lung (bronchus) or breast are by far the commonest of these. Usually the site of the original cancer is known, and the appearance of seizures in such a patient is an ominous sign indicating that a secondary tumour has arisen within the brain. Sometimes, however,

37

the original cancer has not declared itself at the time of the first seizure, and a careful clinical examination will reveal a small tell-tale lump in the breast, or the bronchial cancer will be seen on a chest X-ray.

Primary tumours of the brain never arise in neurones. They either arise in the glia, the supporting cells between neurones playing an active role in their nutrition, or in the meninges, the covering membranes of the brain. These tumours are called gliomas and meningiomas. Subdivisions of gliomas are astrocytomas and oligodendrogliomas — astroyctes and oligodendrocytes being types of glial cells with respectively many and few branching processes. There are other types of primary cerebral tumours, such as those arising from the cells lining the cavities of the brain, or from blood vessels, but these are very rare.

Primary brain tumours are not like cancer of the breast, or bowel or bronchus. They show no tendency to develop blood-borne secondary deposits in other organs. This is fortunate, but there are other characteristics which hinder effective treatment. The gliomas infiltrate normal brain extensively, so there is no apparent margin beyond which one can be quite certain that no abnormal cells have reached. This makes recurrence after surgical excision very likely. Meningiomas, however, are encapsulated tumours, and can often be removed completely, with a good chance of complete eradication. On the converse side, meningiomas are often very vascular tumours, so complete removal may be technically very difficult.

Infectious diseases

Bacterial meningitis can damage the brain at any age from the newborn period to old age. Vigorous and early treatment with antibiotics nearly always prevents damage to the cortex, which lies immediately under the meningeal covering of the brain. However if the treatment is delayed, or the organism is resistant to the antibiotic chosen, the damaged cortical cells may act as seizure foci in subsequent years. Meningitis due to tuberculosis is particularly likely to result in later epilepsy.

A bacterial brain abscess usually now results from blood-borne bacteria which are deposited in the cerebral hemispheres in a patient who is acutely ill with septicaemia. However, most blood-borne bacteria from an infection are filtered out from venous blood as this passes through the capillaries of the lungs. An exception occurs if there is a hole between right and left sides of the heart. Some bacteria may then pass directly from the venous circulation into the left ventricle and into the cerebral circulation. This accounts for the high incidence of cerebral abscess in those with cyanotic heart disease.

An abscess may also form by direct extension into the brain from a local infection — for example severe middle ear suppuration or frontal sinusitis may cause abscesses respectively in the temporal or frontal lobes of the brain.

Acute abscesses can certainly cause epileptic seizures, but, even if successfully treated by drainage and by antiobiotics, further seizures may arise from the scar. In an attempt to avoid this, many surgeons now practice total excision of the capsule of the abscess rather than simple aspiration of the pus.

Viral meningitis is a self-limiting illness, and epilepsy does not occur after this. Sometimes, however, the viruses are present within the substance of the brain, rather than remaining confined to the surface. This is called encephalitis, and seizures may result. One of the commoner viruses causing seizures in this way is the Cytomegalus virus.

Some viruses behave in a very strange way in the brain. Measles, for example, is an illness which affects nearly all children without significant late effects. The illness is terminated by the production of antibodies. A tiny number of children, however, do not succeed in eradicating the virus from their brains, and, some years later a new measles-related illness begins — sub-acute sclerosing pan-encephalitis — in which seizures and mental deterioration are prominent.

39

Epilepsy: the facts

There are other rare encephalopathies caused by viruses. Jakob–Creutzfeldt disease, named after the two men who first described it, is a rare disorder in which seizures and dementia occur, due to an infective agent.

Parasites can also cause epilepsy. The sheep tapeworm *Echinococcus* can, at one stage of its life cycle, enter the bodies of humans who eat contaminated greenstuff such as salads. The next stage of the life cycle is the formation of cysts containing larvae throughout the body, including the brain. The dog tapeworm *Toxocara* has also been incriminated in the development of epilepsy, though with less certain evidence. Toxoplasmosis, possibly acquired through infection *in utero,* is certainly associated with seizures.

Acquired metabolic diseases

The metabolic pathways in the newborn are very unstable and vast changes in the serum concentrations of various ions and metabolites can occur. A blood glucose concentration sufficiently low (hypoglycaemia) to cause seizures, for example, cannot be induced in older children or adults by starvation, or indeed by any means other than the injection of insulin. However severe hypoglycaemia resulting in seizures may be seen in the newborn, particularly in premature infants, or in the babies born to diabetic mothers.

Seizures due to a low serum calcium are also fairly frequent in the newborn period. One cause is early feeding with cow's milk, which is very rich in phosphates, and which results in increased renal excretion of calcium and subsequent hypocalcaemia.

In later stages of life, other acquired metabolic diseases may cause seizures. Chronic renal failure used to be one of the commoner causes, but dialysis and successful transplantation of kidneys has reduced the frequency of seizures due to this cause.

The causes of epilepsy

Alcohol

Alcohol may undoubtedly precipitate seizures in those who already have had previous seizures. This aspect is discussed on page 45. There is also an association between chronic alcohol abuse and the occurrence of fits even when sober. Those who drink alcohol to excess are usually aware that they are running the risk of cirrhosis of the liver, but not many realize that chronic alcoholism can result in loss of cerebral neurones, seizures, and impairment of intellect.

Degenerative disorders

As advances in knowledge occur, fewer and fewer diseases will be assigned to this non-specific group. Jakob–Creutzfeld disease, for example, used to be regarded as such, before it was shown to be due to an infective agent. Pre-senile dementia (Alzheimer's disease), in which the cerebral neurones gradually become fewer in number, is associated with seizures. Almost certainly there is a biochemical abnormality responsible for this loss of neurones, and, hopefully, when this has been identified, some sort of pharmacological treatment will be possible. This sequence of events has already occurred in Parkinson's disease. This was regarded as a degenerative disorder until 15 years ago. A defect in the metabolism of a transmitter called dopamine was identified, and a suitable drug (L-dopa) produced.

How common are the individual causes of epilepsy?

Table 3 shows the causes of epilepsy that could be defined, with a fair degree of confidence, in each of three studies. The way in which the subjects were selected was very different in each study, but the final figure — the proportion in which a cause for epilepsy could be defined — varied within narrow limits, between 20.6 per cent and 26 per cent. Virtually all the subjects in the first two studies had been

41

Table 3. *Identified causes of epilepsy in three studies*

Cause	Per cent	
	Study 1*	Study 2†
Birth trauma and anoxia	2.5	6.3
Cranial injury; post-operative	3.6	7.0
Infections	2.9	3.2
Vascular	5.2	3.2
Tumours	4.1	3.2
Congenital	2.3	1.1
Total	20.6	24.0

Study 3‡
'Uncomplicated epilepsy'   74 per cent
'Epilepsy in association with
    structural brain disorder'   26 per cent

*Hauser and Kurland. Rochester, Minnesota. 516 cases of epilepsy presenting 1935–1967. All ages.
†Hopkins and Scambler. London. 94 cases of epilepsy prevalent in 1973 on the lists of 17 general practitioners. Age over 16.
‡Rutter and colleagues. Isle of Wight. 86 cases of epilepsy prevalent in 1965. Aged 5–14.

investigated with all the techniques then available in major neurological centres.

The fact that three out of four people with epilepsy have no discernible cause for their seizures certainly does not mean that 75 per cent of epilepsy is 'idiopathic' as defined on page 22. From the occurrence of partial seizures originating in one part of the brain, and from focal electroencephalographic abnormalities, Study 2 indicated that there must be a structural though undefined cause for epilepsy in at least 68 per cent of adult subjects. Since the advent of computerized tomography (page 76) we know that a large proportion of subjects with such 'cryptogenic' epilepsy (epilepsy of hidden cause), have minor structural changes in the brain — very commonly zones of atrophy in one or other temporal lobe.

The causes of epilepsy

Precipitants of seizures

Whatever the 'cause', most people with epilepsy analyse their day to day lives in an attempt to detect factors which precipitate seizures.

Virtually every conceivable life event may be blamed by some people with epilepsy, who become overly obsessional about avoiding factors they consider important. For example, one of my patients had each of his two seizures on railway trains. He firmly believes that in some way trains make him have seizures; I believe that this occurrence is just coincidence. Neither of us can be entirely sure that the other is wrong!

There are, however, a number of factors which do seem to precipitate seizures in at least some people with epilepsy.

Sleep and lack of sleep

The electroencephalogram (EEG) is discussed fully on pages 68–76. At this stage, it is only necessary to know that it records the changes in voltage resulting from activity of cerebral neurones. The EEG of people without epilepsy changes during the passage from normal wakefulness, through drowsiness, to sleep. Sleep is not constant, as judged by body movements and EEG patterns, throughout the night. At various intervals one pattern of brain waves occur in association with rapid eye movements. It is during this stage of sleep that dreams occur.

The changing electrical activity of the brain during drowsiness and sleep may allow seizure discharges to 'escape'. Indeed clinical neurophysiologists hope that their patients drop off to sleep during the procedure as the possibility of recording an abnormality is considerably enhanced. Some subjects have all or virtually all the seizures whilst asleep — but they can never be entirely sure that a daytime attack will not occur. A follow-up study of one group of people with 'nocturnal' epilepsy showed that about a third had a daytime seizure in the next five years.

Epilepsy: the facts

Neurophysiological laboratories have investigated the effects of sleep deprivation, either by keeping volunteers continuously awake, or by waking them up every time the EEG showed the pattern of rapid eye movement sleep. In each case EEGs on subsequent undisturbed nights showed that the subjects were catching up on the rapid eye movement sleep they had missed. Deprivation of sleep, therefore, has been shown to alter cerebral electrical activity, and it is not surprising that this is another factor in precipitating seizures. In practical terms, repeatedly staying up late may precipitate seizures in young adults.

Alcohol

One of the commonest reasons for staying up later than usual is to go to a party, where alcohol may be drunk. The social use of alcohol depends largely on its ability to remove inhibiting factors in our personalities and conversation, thereby making us perhaps more interesting and amusing. A similar removal of inhibition of an epileptic focus may allow a seizure to occur. Often, however, the seizure occurs during the 'hang-over', at a time when the blood alcohol is falling, or near zero. It is probable that other changes in body chemistry, particularly in the distribution of water within and outside cells, plays a part in causing such seizures. Over-hydration of experimental animals with epilepsy may precipitate seizures, so there are grounds for believing that large quantities of beer, containing both alcohol and much water, may be more likely to precipitate an attack than moderate use of wine or spirits.

Menstruation

Many women gain three or four pounds weight in the few days preceding their menstrual period. This gain is very largely fluid, manifested by feeling bloated, with distended, sore breasts. Some women with epilepsy, particularly those with partial seizures, may notice an increase in frequency of seizures at the same time. It is not known if water retention is the responsible factor, or whether there is some more complicated hormonal cause. Dehydration with diuretic drugs has been used in attempts to abolish clusters of seizures occurring in relation to menstruation, but with very limited success.

The weight gain associated with oral contraception does not seem to precipitate seizures to any great extent. Oral contraception for women with epilepsy is satisfactory, provided that they understand the interactions between the pill and anticonvulsant drugs explained on page 88.

Stress and worry

It is impossible to quantify stress and worry. Problems perceived as molehills by some may be mountains to others. A period of very hard work at school or office, or a time of emotional unhappiness at home is often associated with an increased number of seizures. A vicious circle may arise, whereby stress and worry precipitate seizures, which in themselves cause further anxiety and hence further seizures. Sometimes an increased number of seizures leads to some crisis in employment, and the anxiety this causes results in a further deterioration in both epilepsy and job prospects.

Mood

Mothers of young children with epilepsy can sometimes tell from their child's mood and behaviour that he is 'building up to a fit'. Adults with epilepsy may experience a peculiar feeling of heaviness or depression on the morning of the days of their seizures. Occasionally elation rather than depression is reported. It is impossible to decide whether these emotional changes cause the seizures, whether both the mood and the seizures are caused by some common factor, or whether the change in mood is in some way produced by a subclinical neuronal discharge that finally erupts into the seizure.

Epilepsy: the facts

Intercurrent illness

Any one with epilepsy may have a seizure in relation to a severe other illness such as pneumonia. In children with epilepsy, fever may precipitate seizures, but it is important to retain the distinction between these and febrile convulsions (pages 143–7).

Drugs

Some chemical compounds are so powerful that they will cause seizures in the majority of those exposed. Pentylene-tetrazol, a war gas, is the primary example, and has been used to induce seizures in those with severe depression as an alternative to electroconvulsive therapy. In this case the seizure is the required effect, but in all other instances seizures complicating drug therapy are very much an unwanted effect.

Antidepressant drugs of the tricyclic group, including amitryptiline (e.g. Tryptizol, Saroten, Domical) and nortryptyline (e.g. Allegron, Aventyl) are amongst those which clearly lower the convulsive threshold and precipitate seizures. Other offenders include phenothiazines, isoniazid, high doses of penicillin, and of course excessive doses of insulin which precipitate seizures through hypoglycaemia. Any of these drugs may precipitate a first seizure or exacerbate established epilepsy. If it is necessary to prescribe an antidepressant for those with epilepsy, viloxazine may be chosen as it probably has the least convulsive effect.

Other drugs may precipitate seizures in those with epilepsy on anticonvulsants by interfering with the metabolism of these drugs.

Finally, it should be remembered that *withdrawal* of some drugs, particularly barbiturates, may precipitate seizures (see page 101).

The causes of epilepsy

Other precipitants — reflex epilepsy

More specific than any of the precipitants so far discussed are the stimuli which result in so-called reflex epilepsy. Figure 12 on page 75 shows the effect of flashing a light in the eyes of a girl aged 16 with this type of epilepsy. In the part of the record shown, flashes at rates of 25 per second produce a wave recorded from the occipital cortex at the back of the brain. These waves follow the flash frequency. As the record proceeds the flash frequency is gradually reduced, and, at a critical frequency, a totally different response of multiple spikes and waves — the *photoconvulsive* response — occurs. In such a child, a seizure may be induced. This of course is a laboratory situation, but seizures may result, in photosensitive children, from flickering light reflected from water, or by the interruption of steady light filtered through trees observed from a moving car.

The commonest type of photosensitivity now encountered is *television epilepsy*. Experiments have shown that it is the normal sweep of the spots that make up the picture from side to side and down the face of the tube that is responsible, and not any malfunction of vertical picture or horizontal line hold. Susceptible children are most at risk when the screen occupies a considerable proportion of the visual field, as will occur if the size of the screen is large, and the child sits close to it, or approaches it to change the programme. The chances of seizures occurring are lessened by sitting far away from the screen. It may also help to reduce contrast between the screen and surroundings by placing the set near a lamp. It has also been shown that the photoconvulsive response cannot be elicited if only one eye is exposed to the flashing light. It makes sense, therefore, for the child to cover one eye if he approaches the set. Remote programme selection is now becoming commonplace, so this facility may be a worthwhile purchase for the parents of a child with photosensitive epilepsy. Both colour and monochrome television sets induce seizures, which are invariably generalized, though they may sometimes be of very short duration — just a few myoclonic jerks of arms and trunk muscles.

Another type of visual reflex epilepsy occurs on looking at patterns such as squares of linoleum tiling. This may be regarded as typical of the highly specific reflex epilepsies occurring in a very few patients in which seizures may be induced by, for example, reading, hearing music (sometimes by only one particular phrase), or by performing mental arithmetic. The perception of such external stimuli must result in a particular pattern of neuronal discharge — this is presumably in part how we recognize tunes and words. One can only imagine that this particular set of neuronal discharge in susceptible people acts as a specific template which, like a key in a lock, unlooses a seizure.

Non-specific stimuli — such as a loud noise, or a startle, however caused, may induce myoclonic jerks, and occasionally a generalized tonic–clonic seizure. This type of epilepsy is seen in some strains of mice, and provides a model for the investigation of the physiology of such seizures.

4

The first seizure and the investigation of epilepsy

Anyone reading this book who has been present at the first grand mal seizure of a child or other relative will remember the sense of shock and feeling of incompetence at coping with a totally unforeseen situation. A common story is for parents to be awoken by the stertorous breathing or grunting of a child in the next bedroom. They go to him, thinking usually that he is having a bad dream, and find him staring, unresponsive, convulsing and perhaps blue. Few if any parents can cope calmly with such a scene. It is usual for the general practitioner to be telephoned at once, and, if there is any delay in his arrival, for an ambulance to be summoned as well. Many parents subsequently confess that they thought their child was dying, so they are acting in an entirely rational way. Almost invariably however, by the time the family doctor or ambulance has arrived, the seizure is over, the child is sleeping peacefully, and the adults are making tea. But they will not sleep again that night. Many — though not all — are immediately aware of the nature of what they have just seen, and all the worries which this book is attempting to put into perspective crowd their minds.

Although the first seizure can occur anywhere and at any time, another common scenario is for the first seizure to occur in a young person in the company of his friends or at work. In this case, the lack of ready access to the family doctor, whose name and telephone number is unlikely to be known to the bystanders, results in an ambulance being almost invariably called, and the unfortunate person being whisked off to hospital. He will recover consciousness either in the ambulance or in the Accident and Emergency Department of the hospital. To the confusion invariably consequent to the generalized seizure must be added the feeling of 'What on earth has happened to me, and how have I finished up here on a stretcher with strangers peering at me?' Obviously, therefore, although ambulance services are rather prickly on this point, a friend should accompany him to hospital — not only to provide moral support when recovery of consciousness occurs but also to give an accurate account of events to the hospital staff. The diagnosis of an epileptic seizure depends very largely on the description of the attack, and important clues about the origin of the seizure may occasionally be obtained from an accurate account, as is discussed on page 55.

What will the doctor do?

What will the family or hospital doctor do immediately after the first attack? He will examine his patient not only just to make sure that eveything is generally weH — for example that breathing is unobstructed — but he will also ascertain if there are any focal neurological signs, which may give him a clue to the cause of the seizure. Though he is not likely to find anything abnormal at this stage, there may be some minor signs such as an asymmetry of the reflexes. He will then question the relatives or other witnesses, and satisfy himself that what has just occurred was indeed a seizure, and not some other event of the type discussed on pages 57–67. Rarely, of course, the first seizure is an early manifestation of an acute and important illness such as meningitis. If he suspects that this might be the case, he will of course arrange immediate admission to hospital. More often, all that is necessary is for him to give a tablet or injection of diazepam (Valium), which is sufficient to raise the seizure threshold and make a second seizure less likely for some hours. This will give everyone time to collect their thoughts and decide on the long-term policy decisions, including the possible needs for referral to a specialist, for investigation and for institution of anticonvulsant treatment.

Epilepsy: the facts

Is referral to a specialist necessary?

The Reid Report on 'People with Epilepsy', published by the British Department of Health and Social Security in 1969, states that: 'The family doctor will undoubtedly wish to refer the majority of his patients for consultant advice, as an epileptic fit is a symptom rather than a disease, and prolonged investigation may be necessary before a firm diagnosis can be reached'. The first clause of this statement is correct. A survey of epilepsy in Metropolitan London, where facilities for neurological consultation are freely available, showed that 95 per cent of all patients had been referred to a hospital for specialist advice. The second clause of this statement is unexceptionable, but the third clause — that perhaps prolonged investigation may be necessary before a firm diagnosis can be reached — inflates, in my view, the problems to unnecessary proportions. From my survey and my experience of hospital and private consulting practice, I believe the majority of referrals occur not because the general practitioner is uncertain as to whether his patient has had a seizure or not, nor because he is seriously concerned about the possibility of serious underlying disease, but for the following reasons.

1. People do not like being told they have had an epileptic seizure. In my experience, and from my survey, I know this difficult task is left to the hospital doctor in about half the cases.

2. People with epilepsy themselves very often feel that some sort of special test is necessary to 'prove' the diagnosis. This point is discussed in relation to electroencephalography on page 76. It must be very difficult to accept the diagnosis, with all its social implications, when it is made on the basis of a 30-second description given to a doctor by a relative or bystander. Somehow it does not seem 'scientific' enough, and yet neurologists place enormous weight on the recounted stories.

3. People with epilepsy are very concerned to discover the 'cause' of their epilepsy. Most think in terms of a single cause,

which, they believe, if eradicated will result in the problem being solved once and for all. Occasionally, of course, an important treatable cause *is* found, and usually special tests are indeed necessary to show this. The difficulty lies in deciding which patients should be so investigated.

4. Traditional medical textbooks have accentuated the unusual and 'interesting' causes of epilepsy, at the expense of the run-of-the-mill patient. General practitioners, educated partly by these books, tend to play safe and refer if referral centres are available.

5. The soundest reason for referral to a neurologist is the complexity of the routes by which he reaches a decision — which he hopes to be correct. This is illustrated in Figure 9. Although I have made the diagram as simple as possible, it illustrates the clarity of thought required to avoid hasty and ill-founded decisions about investigation and treatment. There are three possible preliminary diagnoses: seizure, not

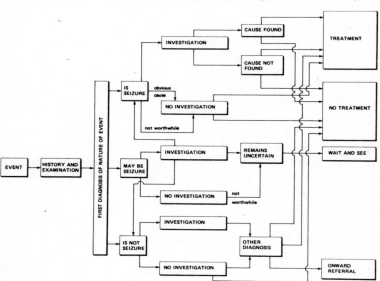

Fig. 9. Decision-making in the management of epilepsy.

seizure, and may be seizure; two policies about investigation; and four possible outcomes: treatment, no treatment, adoption of a wait-and-see policy, and referral to another specialist. For those not used to such networks − or to studying the wiring diagrams of their car, to which Figure 9 bears some similarity − I have numbered 24 possible tracks. There may be more.

I should say that, by the statement in the Figure 'investigation not worthwhile' I mean that a conscious decision is made by the neurologist that investigation is not sufficiently likely to provide a diagnosis to make it worth the subject's time and the nation's expense in investigating the symptoms. An example would be a single seizure in a man of 18 with no physical signs on examination. Few neurologists would think it worthwhile to investigate such a seizure. Another example might be seizures occurring after a known severe head injury; in this case the cause of seizures is obvious.

What will the neurologist do?

The analysis of 'funny turns' or 'blackouts' of one sort or another make up a considerable proportion of the work of a neurologist, so he has experience of navigating the chart shown in Figure 9. His first concern is to obtain as accurate as possible an account of the events which led up to and occurred at the time of a seizure. A person who has lost consciousness cannot himself say what happened while he was unconscious. He will be able to give important information about what he was doing and how he felt before loss of consciousness, and how he felt when he first recovered, but the neurologist will want to know what was happening during the time that consciousness was disturbed. Was he limp or rigid? Were convulsions seen? If so which parts of the body were affected? What colour was he? Did anyone feel his pulse? Was the patient confused when he first recovered? In order that these and other questions be accurately answered, it is essential for the patient to be accompanied to the consultation by anyone who has seen the attack. Such an account is likely to be of far greater value than the results of any test, so every attempt should be made to persuade a friend or relative who saw the 'blackout' that it would be helpful if he could attend the clinic. If this is impossible because of commitments at work, a written description is often of value.

Should consciousness be only partly disturbed, as it may be in partial seizures (see page 20), then the neurologist will listen very carefully to the subjective account of the experiences perceived. There are some points upon which the neurologist will place great accent — a hallucination of an unpleasant odour, for example, or a sense of unreality accompanied by a deep feeling of unnatural fear. Such recounted perceptions will almost certainly lead to a diagnosis of a partial seizure arising in a temporal lobe. There are other phrases, however, of which the neurologist learns to be wary. If the subject says that he 'felt far away', or 'voices sounded far away' during his attack, he may have had a partial epileptic seizure, but such perceptions also occur in the 20 seconds or so preceding a simple faint. In this case the decline in cerebral blood flow, which if continued causes loss of consciousness, produces symptoms which are closely allied to some of those experienced during a partial seizure arising in a temporal lobe.

A logical contradiction may appear to lie in the preceding paragraphs. I have said that an analysis of the story recounted by the patient who has had a blackout is the most powerful tool that a neurologist has in deciding whether that blackout was an epileptic seizure, or some other event such as a faint or other episode of the types discussed on pages 57–67. I have said that investigations do not prove nor disprove the diagnosis. Finally I have said that rather similar perceptions may be experienced during a partial temporal lobe seizure and immediately preceding a faint. How then does a neurologist decide? The answer lies in that woolly statement — 'clinical experience'. What clinical experience means in this context is not only a first-class training but also seeing what happens to patients who have had such symptoms in the next few years. If the patient goes on to have a grand mal seizure, then it is a fair bet that the feelings he experienced some months or years before were also epileptic in nature. By the nature of things, hospital clinics are too busy themselves to follow up at regular intervals all such patients about whom there are grounds for reasonable doubt. The neurologist will convey his doubts to the general practitioner and rely on him to send such a patient back. This small group of subjects, about whom there are grounds for reasonable doubt about the interpretation of recounted events, is one for whom the seeking of a second consultant opinion is occasionally reasonable.

Apart from listening to his patient's account of the blackout itself, the neurologist will ask questions about the circumstances surrounding the attack. For example, was the subject adjusting the television set (page 48) or had he just got out of bed to pass urine (page 59)? Was he on any drugs for other illnesses at that time (page 46)? Had he been drinking (page 45)? These further questions will not only help in accurately distinguishing a seizure from other causes, but may also give him some ideas about how subsequent attacks may be prevented.

The neurologist at this stage will be reasonably confident, in the vast majority of cases, whether he is dealing with a seizure or some other event. Assuming the former, he then will ask a number of questions to decide if there is any obvious clue in previous life to the cause of the seizure. He will enquire about family history of seizures and febrile convulsions, about difficulties in birth and weight at birth, about early development of social and motor skills, about schooling, about the hand favoured in writing, about previous significant illness and about previous head injury. The reasons for doing this are covered on pages 30–41. He will also enquire if there are any recent symptoms such as headache or loss of weight which might indicate that the seizure was due to some advancing cerebral or generalized disease.

The first seizure and the investigation of epilepsy

The neurologist will next examine the patient, often asking him to undress except for underwear. He will begin by feeling the head in case there is any local variation in contour, and, in children, by measuring its circumference. He will then inspect the face, trunk, and limbs for birthmarks that might indicate an associated cerebral lesion. He will examine the eyes using an ophthalmoscope, through which he can see the retina and directly inspect the optic nerve, which may be swollen in rare cases of epilepsy. He will also examine the field of vision and eye movements. He will be interested in any asymmetry in the face or bulk of the limbs which might indicate some long-standing brain damage sustained in infancy. He will also detect any difference in muscle tone or power, and any asymmetry between the tendon reflexes. He will vigorously scratch the sole of the foot. This normally produces downward flexion of the big toe. An upward move-ment may indicate brain damage. He will then examine the cardiovascular system — the pulse for irregularity, the blood pressure, which may be elevated, and the heart and neck and skull for murmurs. He will feel the abdomen to ensure that there are no enlarged organs.

Having then finished his interview with his patient and friends, and examined his patient, the neurologist will collect his thoughts. He may be certain that he is dealing with one or more epileptic seizures; he may be certain that he is dealing with some other explanation for attacks or blackouts; he may remain uncertain at this stage as to whether the patient has had seizures.

Causes of attacks and blackouts other than epilepsy

Obviously the first necessity in the management of epilepsy is to ensure that the events described are indeed epileptic seizures, and not some other type of attack or blackout. We therefore now have to consider other events that might be confused with seizures.

Epilepsy: the facts

Diminution in cerebral blood flow

This is the mechanism common to a number of different causes of disturbances of consciousness.

Simple faints. The medical name for these is syncope. Many of us have experienced one or more syncopal attacks, very often at school. In syncope, consciousness is disturbed or lost, not because of a paroxysmal discharge of cerebral neurones, but because the cerebral neurones are silenced by inadequate supply of oxygen through arterial blood.

When a man stands up, his brain is about 15 inches (38 cm) higher than his heart; when he lies down, the two organs are at the same level. When he stands up, therefore, the arterial pressure has to increase so that blood continues to reach the brain. Normally, this is accompanied smoothly by a combination of increased heart rate and by constriction of the blood vessels in the abdomen and legs. Experience informs us of examples of a breakdown in this mechanism. The most familiar is the extreme slowing of the heart-rate produced in some sensitive people by the sight of blood or in response to pain. This cardiac slowing is mediated through the vagal nerve, and the name vaso-vagal attack is often given to such an episode. The contraction of leg and thigh muscles during walking normally drives venous blood back to the heart. If venous return is insufficient because of immobility − for example a soldier at attention on parade, or a young girl in Assembly at school − then syncope may occur. Such syncope seems to be socially infectious − once one girl or soldier has slumped, others may follow in the next few minutes.

Normally blood returns to the heart from the legs smoothly through the chest and abdomen. During prolonged coughing, or straining at stool, the pressure within the chest is greatly increased, preventing venous return to the heart. What the heart is not getting back, it cannot put out, so this sequence of events again may result in impaired blood-flow to the brain, and syncope.

58

The first seizure and the investigation of epilepsy

If the blood vessels in trunk and legs are pleasantly dilated in a hot bath or nice warm bed, suddenly getting up — for example, to answer the telephone — may cause syncope. This may also happen in older people, when they get out of bed at night to pass urine. The situation is more complex in this case because we know that, at the onset of urination, there is a reflex dilation of blood vessels in the legs. This so-called 'micturition syncope' affects men more than women, not only because they more often have to pass urine at night, because of prostatic enlargement, but because they pass urine standing up.

Syncope may occur in association with certain diseases. For example, in diabetes the nerve fibres controlling the heart and diameter of blood vessels may be diseased, and the normal adjustments to blood pressure to posture may fail to occur. There are other rare diseases of the brain in which a similar failure to control blood pressure occurs. One, which bears some similarity to Parkinson's disease, is known as the Shy–Drager syndrome after the two American neurologists who first described it.

A much commoner cause of syncope, however, is medication. Many people take tablets to control high blood pressure. One effect of some of these drugs is to cause syncope on standing up. Some antidepressants, such as imipramine (Tofranil), do the same.

How does the neurologist decide that his patient's blackouts are due to syncope rather than epilepsy? Again, all depends upon the story. The first clue is the circumstances in which the blackout occurred. If it happened at the scene of a road accident, or during a horror movie, syncope is very likely. A common story now is for a man to faint while attending his wife's delivery! Syncope virtually never occurs lying down, so if loss of consciousness happens then a seizure is very likely. Very occasionally, vagal slowing of the heart can be so profound that syncope *does* happen lying down. For example, one of my patients was a woman who was so terrified of dental treatment that she lost consciousness even if the dentist started treating her with the chair tilted back to the horizontal position.

The next point is the occurrence of pre-syncopal symptoms. Blood flow to the brain is reduced in syncope for often many seconds before consciousness is lost. During that time, the nervous system makes desperate attempts to constrict peripheral blood vessels in order to elevate the central pressure. The constriction of blood vessels in the skin results in pallor, and the associated discharge of the vegetative (non-voluntary) nervous system causes nausea and sweating. The subject therefore feels and looks cold, pale, and clammy.

Other points which help distinguish syncope from seizures include limpness, rather than rigidity and/or convulsions during the period of unconsciousness, and an absence of incontinence during the event. Recovery of full consciousness and orientation is much more rapid after syncope than after a seizure, following which there is usually a period of confusion. Recovery after syncope often rapidly follows assumption of the horizontal position, whether the subject falls, or is placed like this, so that the head is on the same level as the heart. This is nature's safety mechanism whereby cerebral blood flow is restored. Occasionally the safety mechanism cannot operate – the position of a hand-basin or lavatory may prevent the limp body falling to the floor. Sometimes the sufferer is supported in a vertical position by well-meaning but ill-advised friends or bystanders. In this case cerebral blood flow may fall to such extremely low levels that incontinence, twitching, or a full-blown seizure may occur. This should be regarded as an 'anoxic seizure' rather than a seizure due to epilepsy.

As an example of the difficulties that this unusual sequence of events can cause, I was asked to see a young nurse at the hospital at which I work. Three days after a straight-forward appendicectomy, she got up for the first time to go to the ward lavatory. She felt faint as she walked there, and therefore left the door ajar. She felt fainter still as she was sitting on the seat, straining to open her bowels. Before losing consciousness she called another nurse for help. This girl, seeing her colleague about to tumble off the seat, held her up to prevent injury. The resulting cerebral anoxia caused a seizure. Before I was asked to see her an incorrect diagnosis of epilepsy had been made, and her continued employment as a nurse was under threat.

Syncope in adolescents — usually girls — can be very troublesome, and occasional injury occurs. Although the stereotype sufferer is a thin, delicate, boy-friendless bookworm, I seem to see just as many horse-riding, jolly-hockey-stick girls with syncope, so the usual advice to take plenty of fresh air and exercise is probably useless. Much more important is to tell the girl to lie down *at once* if she fells the onset of typical pre-syncopal symptoms. Fortunately recurrent episodes are rarely troublesome for more than a year.

Breathholding attacks. These attacks occur only in young children, aged mostly between one and two years. The typical story is of a child who is crossed in some way, so he becomes suddenly angry, or upset. In other children, attacks occur if they are unexpectedly hurt or frightened. The child cries vigorously once or twice, and then holds his breath at the end of one expiration. After a few seconds he becomes blue from lack of oxygen in the blood (cyanotic), and then loses consciousness. He is limp, but one or two jerks may follow.

The mechanism seems to be similar to that of syncope associated with coughing (page 58). The sharp rise in pressure within the chest prevents return of blood to the heart and so cardiac output and cerebral blood flow fall.

Sometimes the child is not cyanosed, but just pale and limp. In these cases, it is believed that there is a short, but not dangerous, period during which the heart is hardly beating at all for a few seconds. It is not uncommon for children with breathholding attacks to be diagnosed as having epilepsy. The association with frustration, rage, or a sudden hurt is the most useful pointer to the correct diagnosis. No medication helps. The child will always breathe again spontaneously. Attacks cease by the age of four or five — perhaps when the child has sufficient language for rational discourse rather than rage!

Disturbances of cardiac rhythm (cardiac dysrhythmia). Disturbance of consciousness in syncope is due to failure of blood supply to the brain, due in part to a fall in cardiac output. Cardiac output may also be less than normal if the rhythm of the heart is abnormal. Both very slow and very fast heart rates diminish cardiac output.

The distinction of a disturbance of consciousness due to a cardiac dysrhythmia from a seizure is not easy. Occasionally, though, a bystander will note that someone is pulseless or has a very irregular pulse during the attack, and sometimes the sufferer himself notices palpitations before disturbance of consciousness. Cardiac rhythm is easily monitored by electrocardiography. The change in voltage associated with contraction of the different chambers of the heart are of sufficient amplitude that they can easily be recorded on a cassette recorder for periods of 24 hours, and their occurrence in relation to symptoms analysed. In some studies, a cardiac cause for disturbance of consciousness was found in up to one quarter of cases first presenting to neurological clinics.

Localized diminution in cerebral blood flow. The changes in blood flow that we have considered so far in our differential diagnosis have affected all parts of the brain equally. In older people, atheromatous (arteriosclerotic) changes take place in the arteries in the neck and head. There may be a temporary blockage of an artery to one part of the brain by a fragment of atheroma swept downstream from a larger artery by the flow of blood. Neurologists call these 'transient ischaemic attacks'. In some of these short episodes, muscle weakness or tingling in one or other limb may slightly resemble focal motor or sensory seizures (page 17). However, although focal motor

62

seizures may arise in the scarred brain in the territory of a *permanently* blocked artery (page 35), the *transient* ischaemic attacks are associated with transient paralysis rather than convulsions.

In younger people, localized (focal) neurological phenomena occur in *migraine*. In the first stage of a classical migraine attack, arterial spasm occurs, reducing cerebral blood flow focally. The occipital area is the region most often affected. This results in a hallucination of distorted vision or flashing lights, rather than the formed visual hallucination which may be part of a partial seizure arising in a temporal lobe. Occasionally spasm affects the motor or sensory areas of the brain, producing short-lived paralysis or disturbance of sensation, without convulsions, on the opposite side of the body.

Narcolepsy

Any one of us may feel drowsy in a stuffy lecture theatre, or as a passenger on a long car journey. Those suffering from narcolepsy, however, feel an uncontrollable desire to sleep at other times, and may indeed drop off in socially embarrassing circumstances. This unusual symptom may be associated with 'cataplexy' — a sudden loss of postural tone causing collapse without loss of consciousness, often precipitated by strong emotions such as anger or amusement. In a way, these phenomena are nearest to epilepsy, as they presumably result from some paroxysmal disorder of cerebral neurones. However, such patients have epileptic seizures no more often than the general population, the electroencephalogram whilst awake is always normal, and drugs of a completely different type from those used in epilepsy may produce a favourable response.

Drop attacks

These affect only middle-aged women, and then often only

for a year or two. The story is very striking. The woman complains that, while walking along, she suddenly finds that her legs have given way. She may land on her knees or pitch forward on to her face. In either case she is always adamant that she is fully aware of what is happening, and equally adamant that she does not trip. The condition is variously assumed to be due to some weakness of the thigh muscles, or to a disturbance of blood flow in the brain-stem, interfering with postural reflexes. Whatever the mechanism, neurologists are confident that there is no association with epilepsy.

Jumping legs (myoclonic jerks)

About 80 per cent of the adult population, at some time in their lives, are conscious of a sudden jerk of one or other leg, usually in the twilight stage of drifting off to sleep. The jerk is associated with, or may cause, a sudden arousal. Some people have a great number of jerks, so many that their spouse, being bruised by the kicks, will refuse to share a bed with them. These jerks must, I think, represent some sort of paroxysmal discharge of neurones, not necessarily in the brain. They are therefore in this way close to epilepsy, but are not so regarded because of their near universality in the population, and their lack of association with frank epileptic seizures. Specifically, there is no relation between these jerks and the morning myoclonic jerks associated with petit mal (page 17).

Vertigo

Doctors are careful to distinguish true vertigo — a perception of dysequilibrium of the body in its relation to space — from non-specific feelings in the head such as 'dizziness' or 'muzziness' which are so often associated with anxiety and depression. True vertigo is rarely a symptom of a partial seizure in a temporal lobe. Far more common is vertigo due to a disorder of the balancing organ — the labyrinth — lying within the inner ear. The labyrinth may malfunction in an episodic way in both children and adults. In young children the distinction between paroxysmal vertigo and partial seizures may not be easy, as in both the child is frightened, and may either hold on to his mother or fall. The distinction rests on the absence of amnesia or confusion after the attack of benign paroxysmal vertigo, and the presence of abnormal tests of labyrinthine function.

Rigors

Occasionally the shivering associated with high fever, particularly frequent in infections of the urinary tract, may be confused with a convulsion.

Night terrors

It is very upsetting for parents, settling down for their own night's sleep, to be disturbed by terrifying screams from their child. When they go to him, they find him sitting up in bed, wide-eyed and unresponsive to their questions. Within a few seconds, however, he will lie down, turn over, resume sleep, and have no recollection of the event the next morning. Though it is natural for parents to brood darkly on what school is doing to their darling, night terrors may affect the happiest children, and the condition is not associated with any long-term emotional disturbance. The only reason why night terrors should be confused with seizures is ther unexpectedness, the way the house can be thrown into confusion, and the unresponsiveness of the child to his parents' attempts to comfort him.

Tics, habits and ritualistic movements

Tics in children usually involve the upper part of the face — screwing up the eyes, or rapid blinking. More complex habits such as grunting, and brushing the hair away from the eyes are common in children, and seldom confused with seizures. Sometimes, however, children indulge in strange patterns of movement which they apparently find pleasurable, and which they stop immediately on reprimand. Sometimes infants and toddlers will rock backwards and forwards squeezing their thighs together in a manner which seems to be masturbatory.

Overbreathing

Breathing in and out too fast and too deep is one bodily way in which, like palpitations, anxiety is manifested. This response seems to be particularly common in adolescent girls. If continued for more than a few minutes, excessive carbon dioxide is removed by the lungs from the blood, which becomes correspondingly alkaline. This affects the levels of ionized calcium in the blood, and, in turn, the conduction of nerve impulses and the contraction of muscles. The net effect is that the subject experiences painful tingling in the hands and toes, which become flexed and contracted in a cramped posture. The lack of carbon dioxide also produces a feeling of light-headedness, and the total picture may be confused with a seizure. Treatment is simple and dramatically effective. A paper or polythene bag is placed (temporarily!) over the patient's head, so that she re-breathes her own expired air, rich in carbon dioxide. The body chemistry and clinical state rapidly return to normal.

Simulated seizures

It might seem strange that anyone would wish to pretend to have an epileptic seizure, but in consultant practice this is one of the commoner differential diagnoses to be considered. The great majority of such patients have some knowledge of epilepsy − either they have seen a relative with seizures, or more commonly they have had some true seizures themselves. Unless the true and suspect attacks are both seen by an expert, it may be impossible to sort out exactly what is happening. A doctor may be trapped into giving more and more anticonvulsant drugs for seizures which he believes to be out of control. Conversely if he sees one fit which he is quite sure is feigned, he may well wrongly believe all are feigned.

The points which distinguish a true and simulated seizure are the character of the convulsions, which are often not imitated very well. A colleague (David Marsden) has rightly remarked that they are 'intensified by restraint and mollified by inattention'. Incontinence does not distinguish between true and simulated seizures as this can be, and often is, simulated. A normal electroencephalogram recorded during a generalized 'seizure' is virtually incontrovertible evidence of simulation. However, the records may be so technically marred by the patient's thrashing around that interpretation is difficult.

Psychiatrists, rightly or wrongly, draw a distinction between simulation of disease due to conscious malingering, for example a man pretending to be sick to avoid conscription to the Army, and unconscious hysteria, in which it is alleged that the simulation is the product of the unconscious mind. In each case some potential gain to the patient from the pretence is apparent. The gain in simulating seizures usually is to seek more attention. Rather than lay blame, doctors should regard these events as an indication that the patient cannot cope with his life's problems.

The investigation of seizures

There are three reasons for the investigation of seizures: to improve the certainty with which the diagnosis is made, to ascertain the type of seizure (important when considering choice of medication and prognosis), and to ascertain the cause of seizures.

Epilepsy: the facts

Electroencephalography (EEG)

Electroencephalography is the principal investigation available to improve the certainty of diagnosis and ascertain the seizure type. As I have already written on page 54, I regard an account of the seizure itself as of first importance, but electroencephalography is a useful tool in some cases.

As described on page 2, a neurone maintains a small voltage charge across its cell membrane. The neurone signals to others with which it is connected by discharging this voltage. The voltage charge, although small — about 75-thousands of a volt — is big enough to be easily recorded by an electrode in close proximity to the cell, or within the cell itself. Much of the recent advances in neurophysiology over the last 40 years have come from such studies on animal brains and spinal cord.

It is of course ethical and practical to insert electrodes into human brains only in rare and exceptional circumstances. The further the electrode is away from the cell, the harder it is to detect voltage changes. Just like gravity, the 'signal' varies as the square of the distance. It was very much to everyone's surprise, therefore, that an Austrian psychiatrist called Hans Berger claimed, in 1929, to be able to record electrical signals from the brain using electrodes placed on the surface of the scalp. This was long before the days of transistors, and the thermionic valve had only come into use shortly before. Berger's equipment was primitive, by our standards, and unstable. It was therefore first assumed by Berger's detractors that the wavy lines he produced were fluctuations in the base line of the instrument's sensitivity, rather than true signals from the brain. However, the English neurophysiologist, Adrian, soon confirmed Berger's observations, and electroencephalography as a clinical investigation was born. Advances in electronics have since been so enormous that the voltage signals can be detected and recorded with ease. Unfortunately the understanding and interpretation of the records has not kept pace.

The first seizure and the investigation of epilepsy

All hospitals with neurological and neurosurgical units, and some larger non-specialized hospitals will have facilities for recording electroencephalograms. The procedure is quite painless. Some people still confuse the *recording* of electrical signals by the EEG with the *giving* of electroconvulsive therapy, so it is important that the technician reassures the subject that he is only recording 'what's already there', and that he is not putting anything in. After this reassurance, the technician's first job is to measure up his patient's head for correct placement of this electrodes. Virtually all units now use the International system of electrode placement, in which measurements are taken from the root of the nose, and the protuberance at the back of the head. The electrodes themselves are either little silver discs, which are fastened to the head with a sticky substance known as collodion, or gauze pads moistened with saline. Considerable adjustment may be necessary to get correct positions, and good contact with low electrical resistance. Wires leading from the electrodes are connected to sockets on a 'headbox' and this in turn is connected by a cable to the EEG machine (Plate 2). Inside this are a series of amplifiers, the final stages of which are sufficiently powerful to deflect between eight and twenty pens or ink-jets in directions corresponding to the original voltage changes occurring within the brain. The pens or ink-jets write on paper that is moving under them at a fixed speed, usually three centimetres per second. The signals may also be tape-recorded for subsequent replay and, perhaps, computer analysis.

Not all the electrodes feed their signals into the machine at once. The technician can use the switches on the machine to choose various combinations, known as montages. In Figure 10, for example, the top trace is recording the voltage change between electrodes known as Fp2 and F8.

In the course of the recording the technician will ask his patient to do a number of things. First of all, the subject must not fidget or move about, or the electrical activity of muscle will swamp that of brain. From time to time, he will

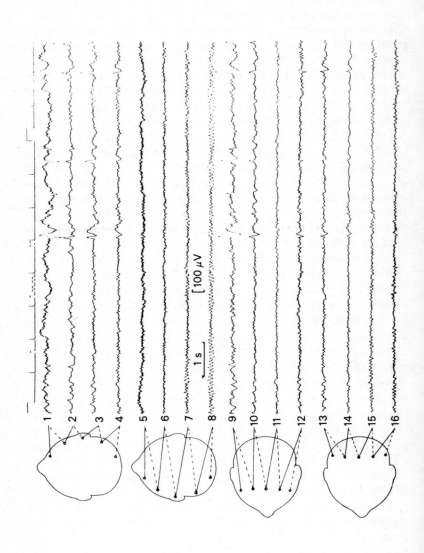

be asked to open and close his eyes, as this manoeuvre should, in a normal brain, produce definite changes in the basic rhythm recorded from the back of the head. This so-called α-rhythm has a basic frequency of 9–11 cycles per second. In Figure 10, it can be seen most clearly in trace 8. It is reduced in amplitude or abolished by opening the eyes. Like all other voltage changes recorded from scalp electrodes, it is not produced by the discharges of single cells, but by voltage fluctuations in enormous populations of cells in some sort of synchrony.

While recording the background rhythm from the occipital, temporal, parietal, and frontal regions of the brain, the technician will be watching the moving paper not only for variations in these basal rhythms, but also looking out for abnormal discharges. In epilepsy, these may be of various types.

One of the most striking examples is illustrated in Figure 10. This EEG was recorded from a girl aged 13 who had begun to experience brief blank spells lasting two to three seconds about two years before. Subsequently more prolonged dreamy states occurred, in assocation with twitching of the left arm. Traces 1, 2, 3, 9, and 10 all show the occurrence of a spike, followed by a slow wave occurring three times in the ten seconds of record shown. From this knowledge of the electrode positions, indicated diagrammatically on the left of the record, it can be seen that all the traces which show the spike are derived from electrodes on the right side of the head, from the scalp overlying the anterior temporal lobe. The spikes in traces 1 and 2 are virtually mirror images. This so called phase reversal between the two traces indicates that the abnormal discharge is propagated from a point in close proximity to the electrode common to both traces.

Fig. 10. Electroencephalogram (EEG) of girl aged 13 with temporal lobe epilepsy. The diagrams on the left of the record indicate the positions of the electrodes on the scalp in relation to the nose and ears. See text for further description.

71

Epilepsy: the facts

On this occasion, the recordist was lucky in that a definite spike discharge occurred during the recording. He might have only recorded traces similar to the apparently rather featureless traces seen in the left hand side — the first four seconds — of the record shown. However, close inspection shows that even this section shows clear-cut abnormalities. Compare traces 2 and 6 for example, derived from equivalent electrodes on the right and left side of the head. Trace 2 shows irregular slow waves which are abnormal, occurring with a frequency of about 4 cycles per second, totally absent from trace 6. Compare also traces 4 and 8. The normal α-rhythm at 11 cycles per second seen over the left side of the back of the head is missing over the right side. It is on these more subtle asymmetries that much depends.

If there is no striking abnormality during the record, the recordist will encourage the subject to relax and, if possible, to fall asleep. Drowsiness and sleep may release discharges not present in the record whilst awake. Another technique to 'activate' the record is overbreathing (hyperventilation). Figure 11 shows the effect of this. The subject was an eight-year-old girl who had begun to have blank spells lasting two or three seconds about one year before. The first part of the record had shown no abnormality, and she was instructed to breathe in and out heavily. After doing this for about 2½ minutes a sudden burst of large-amplitude spikes followed by slow waves occurred symmetrically in all traces derived from all parts of the scalp. The complexes of spikes and slow waves occurred at a frequency of 3 cycles per second. Consciousness was disturbed during this episode which lasted for about 10 seconds. The evidence for this is that she spontaneously stopped overbreathing during the discharge, and resumed thereafter. This is a typical (petit mal) absence, only distinguished from the blank spells of the 13-year-old girl described above by electroencephalography. Accurate classification of seizure types, with a view to the choice of anticonvulsants, is one of the most useful roles for the EEG.

Another method of activating abnormalities in the EEG is

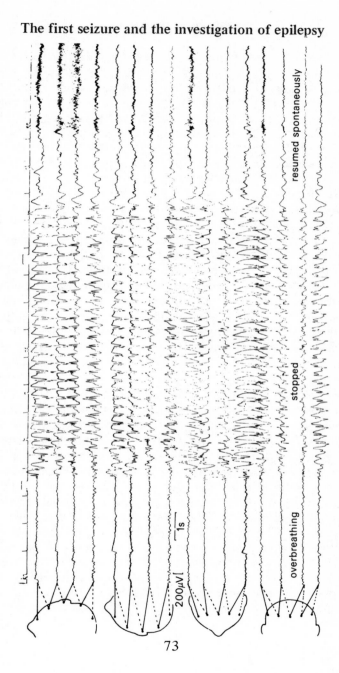

73

Fig. 11. EEG of girl aged 8 with typical absence attacks. See text for further description.

photic stimulation. Figure 12 is the EEG of a girl aged 16. She and her three siblings all have myoclonic seizures, some of which are precipitated by exposure to light. In this record, trace 10 shows the frequency of flash of a stroboscopic light held in front of her eyes. The resting record is normal, as is the first few seconds of exposure to flash. The initial flash frequency is 25 per second, but as it declines to 18 per second a symmetrical paroxysmal discharge begins which outlasts exposure to the flash.

The three records chosen for illustration all have striking abnormalities, but the records of many people with undoubted epilepsy are not detectably different from the range of variation seen in healthy people. In our survey of epilepsy in London, we found that, of 72 people with undoubted epilepsy who had had one or more EEGs that we could review, normal EEGs or EEGs showing trivial and uninformative abnormalities had been obtained in 38. Of course the longer the recording, and the more vigorous the activating techniques, the more likely it is that some clear-cut abnormality will emerge. However, it is not often that these more vigorous efforts result in a change in management.

Advances in electronic instrumentation over the last few years have allowed prolonged EEG recording while the subject is about his normal activities. The electrical signals detected by the scalp electrodes can be fed into a portable cassette tape recorder for subsequent replay and analysis, or the signals can be converted into radio waves and beamed to an observer with a tape recorder some metres distant. This technique allows the subject to carry out his normal activities free from trailing wires. The technical problems are, however, considerable. The technique is most useful for those who are currently having attacks the nature of which is poorly understood. If it is combined with video recording of behaviour during the attacks, a replay of the video tape and EEG tape in synchrony may allow a correct analysis of events.

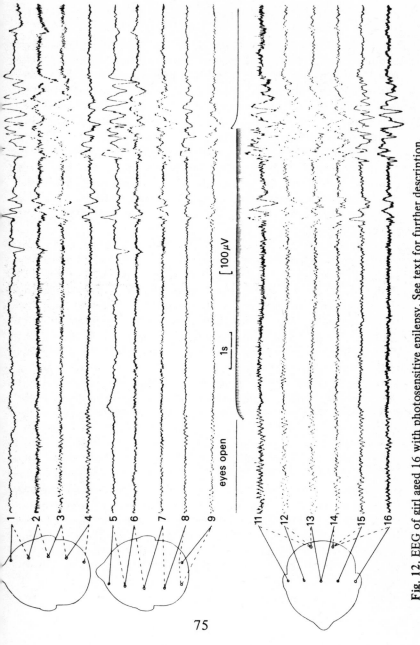

Fig. 12. EEG of girl aged 16 with photosensitive epilepsy. See text for further description.

75

Epilepsy: the facts

The EEG is not a good guide to the activity of epilepsy. For example, one patient, a boy of 12, has had a continuous right frontal discharge, which has been present in four EEGs recorded during the last three years. The boy has had repeated partial seizures from the age of six to nine years, but has had none during the last three years, in spite of this continuing abnormality.

It has also been shown that the EEG is not a good prognostic indicator for the later development of epilepsy after trauma, nor a reliable indicator of the likelihood of relapse on termination of treatment. Its role, therefore, is a limited one, but, properly used, it sometimes gives information not otherwise available.

It must be clearly understood that the EEG does not prove, nor disprove the diagnosis of epilepsy. As already stated, a record can be normal in someone with undoubted epilepsy. There is always the danger that a doctor, hovering on the brink of making a diagnosis of epilepsy, may be tipped into making a 'definite' diagnosis of epilepsy by the presence of marginal abnormalities on the EEG. If the record shows clear-cut paroxysmal activity, then this lends considerable support to the diagnosis. If the record shows only a minor excess of slower rhythms, and the report reads that the record is 'compatible with epilepsy', then the doctor and his patient are no further forward in establishing any diagnosis.

Computed axial tomography

The EEG is the best available method of recording seizure discharges; it is a measure of cerebral function. Cerebral structure, on the other hand, is best demonstrated by the technique of computed axial tomography – often abbreviated to CAT or CT scanning. The abbreviation EMI scanning is also often used after the initials of the company whose scientist, Hounsfield, developed and introduced the technique. Examples of CT scans are shown in Plate 1 in the middle of this book. The technique depends upon the fact that different tissues absorb different amounts of X-rays. In principle, a detector between the X-ray emitting tube and the head measures the quantity of X-ray photons going into the head in one axis, and another detector measures the quantity coming out on the other side. A small computer stores the difference in its memory. The X-ray tube and the detectors are then rotated round the head by one degree and the process repeated. The absorption of X-rays at each point within the examined 'slice' of the head can then be calculated by the computer on the basis of the stored differences in absorption. The X-ray absorptions can be presented as numbers on a printout, but for clinical purposes the computer is programmed to display a spot on a television tube, the location of which represents the location within the brain slice, and the intensity of which represents the degree of X-ray absorption.

In Plate 1, the bone of the skull, which absorbs a lot of X-ray photons, is represented by the white ring, around a greyer brain. Cerebrospinal fluid, which absorbs fewer photons than brain, is black, so that the ventricles of the brain, which contain the fluid, are clearly outlined. Cerebral scars, infarcts, and cysts are less dense than normal brain, and so show up as darker areas than normal. Tumours are often denser, or 'whiter' than normal brain. Their density can be enhanced by intravenous injection of a simple compound containing iodine. Iodine absorbs many X-ray photons, and as it tends to leak from the circulation at the site of a tumour, the absorption of X-rays in the neighbourhood of the tumour will be increased.

CT scanning is such a powerful technique that its use will probably become more and more routine in the investigation of epilepsy. Already, in those centres where it has been widely used, it has confirmed the belief that idiopathic epilepsy (see page 22) is rare, and minor structural abnormalities, unrevealed by earlier techniques, are the cause of most cases of epilepsy. At present, the cost of buying, installing, and running a machine precludes its use in the more straightforward cases of epilepsy. The management of temporal lobe epilepsy, for example, is not altered by the demonstration of a small scar in one or other temporal lobe.

Other radiological investigations

Before the advent of CT scanning, the ventricles of the brain were vizualized by outlining them by air, introduced through a lumbar puncture needle. The difference in X-ray absorption between air and brain is so great that the ventricles could be readily demonstrated using photographic methods of recording absorption. This procedure – known as air encephalography – usually resulted in a headache for a day or two, and was extremely time-consuming. It is still done in some special cases prior to operation, but its use has greatly declined since the introduction of CT scanning.

Another technique, arteriography, is still widely used in those patients with epilepsy due to a structural cause such as a tumour or angioma, and for whom surgery is being considered (Plate 2). In this technique an iodine-containing solution, which densely absorbs X-rays, is injected directly into one or other carotid artery, or through a catheter introduced into the brachial or femoral arteries, and passed into the region of the carotid. Immediately after the injection a series of X-ray photographs are taken, the arteries and veins being outlined by the radio-dense material. This technique has the advantage of informing the neurosurgeon of the exact position of those abnormal arteries and veins he may encounter at operation.

An ordinary X-ray of the skull may provide useful information in someone with epilepsy. It may show a minor asymmetry of the skull not apparent on clinical examination. In an adult, this would suggest that the cause of epilepsy had been present during the years of childhood in which the shape of the skull is formed. Calcification may be seen within the skull in rare cases, due to abnormalities of calcium

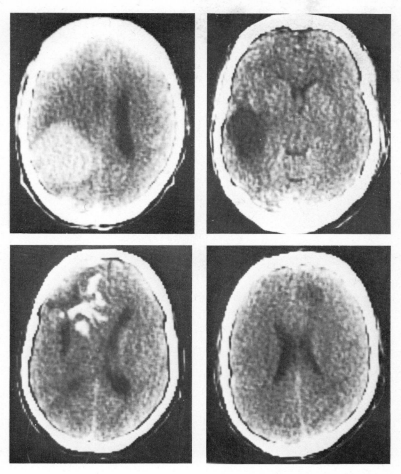

PLATE 1. Computed axial cranial X-ray tomography of the brains of subjects with abnormalities giving rise to epilepsy. In each case the curved dark shadows in the middle of the photographs are the ventricles of the brain.

Top left: The white circle is a meningioma (see page 37) in the left parietal lobe.

Top right: The dark circular area is an old scar caused by a stroke, in the left mid-temporal region.

Bottom left: The white irregular patch is a glioma (see page 37) in the left frontal region.

Bottom right: The dark circular area turned out to be a right frontal glioma.

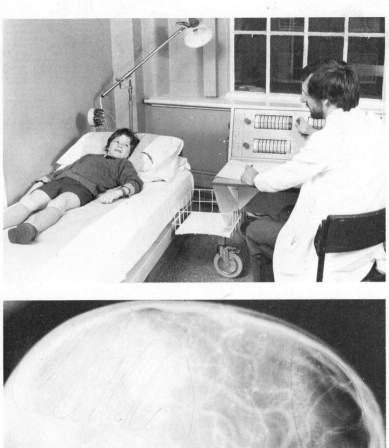

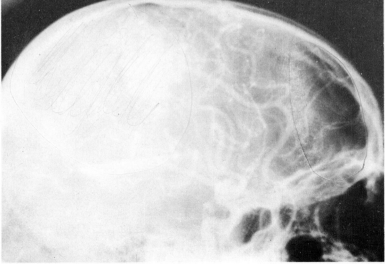

PLATE 2. *Top:* The recording of an electroencephalogram (EEG)
Bottom: Demonstration of abnormal blood vessels by arteriogram (page 78). Middle cerebral artery supplying arteriovenous malformation (angioma; page 33) (white area at top of plate).

metabolism, tuberose sclerosis, angiomas, parasites, or tumours.

Doctors will arrange a chest X-ray in smokers who develop epilepsy over the age of about forty, in case their seizures are due to a secondary deposit from a cancer of the bronchus.

Lumbar puncture

In someone who develops seizures in the presence of an acute neurological illness such as meningitis, lumbar puncture is an essential early investigation. However, although often done by non-neurologists, it is only very rarely needed in the investigation of epilepsy *per se*. It may be required if syphilis or some other chronic low-grade infection of the nervous system is suspected.

Blood tests

Abnormalities of glucose, calcium, magnesium, or amine metabolism in young children may be detected by estimating these substances in the blood, but it is unusual for blood tests to be helpful in elucidating the cause of adult epilepsy. A 'surprise' blood alcohol estimation is sometimes revealing, as is a test for syphilis.

Biopsy

Removal of tissue for microscopic analysis may be helpful in rare causes of epilepsy. Biopsy of the skin abnormalities associated with tuberose sclerosis or neurofibromatosis may confirm a previously suspected diagnosis. A sample of neurones can be directly and harmlessly obtained by biopsy of the rectal wall; this is very useful in confirming some of the lipid storage diseases of children. Direct biopsy of the brain is only very rarely resorted to in neurological practice as it is seldom that management is affected, and the procedure is not without risk. I do not think it would be justified in the investigation of epilepsy.

All in all, therefore, investigation of seizures has a limited value. An EEG may rarely improve the certainty of diagnosis, though it often helps ascertain the type of seizure, and so aids the correct choice of anticonvulsant drug. CT scanning will give a direct visual demonstration of the structural abnormality causing seizures, though this does not often influence management. Simple blood tests and skull X-rays, though cheap to perform, seldom show a relevant abnormality. With this knowledge, the neurologist will often embark upon few if any investigations. His perspective may be that he is faced with a problem that is common in his practice, and that there are well recognized and effective policies for coping with the matter. A good and kind neurologist will recognize that this professional perspective, based on his knowledge and experience, is not that of his patient, who is frightened and bewildered by the onset of events which he does not understand, but which he feels may have important effects on his life and career.

The technical aspects of the neurological consultation — the history, the differential diagnosis, the examination, any necessary investigation, and prescription of anticonvulsant — take comparatively little time. Most of the consultation should be spent, in my view, in exploring the subject's attitudes and knowledge about epilepsy, and the effect that epilepsy may have on his life, so that practical advice and support can be given. Often this may take more than one consultation. How much of this support should be provided by the neurologist and how much by the family doctor depends upon the personalities of the doctors and the patient, as well as upon the available time. What *is* disastrous for the patient is if each doctor assumes that the other is coping with these aspects.

5

Treatment

All people with epilepsy agree that the aim of treatment is absolute abolition of seizures. Anything less is very much second best. One or two seizures a year cause almost as many problems with regard to work and personal relationships as do a couple of dozen.

Methods of seizure control include:
- avoidance of precipitants of seizures
- anticonvulsant drugs
- modification of diet
- surgery
- repeated stimulation of the cerebellum by implanted electrodes
- biofeedback

Each method will now be discussed — but before any reader with epilepsy becomes excited by the thoughts of treatments he has so far not experienced, he should know that it is only in unusual circumstances that methods other than the first two are employed or found to be useful.

Avoidance of precipitants of seizures

Precipitants of seizures are discussed on pages 43–9. When there is a clear precipitant such as television, then common sense dictates how the effect may be minimized. It is difficult to avoid the less clear-cut though undoubtedly important precipitants such as anxiety and stress.

Anticonvulsant drugs

All sorts of pills and potions have been used to treat epilepsy throughout the history of medicine. Those interested in a fuller account should read *The falling sickness* by Oswei Temkin (Johns Hopkins Press, Baltimore, 1945) and *Epilepsy and related disorders* by William Lennox (Little Brown, Boston, 1960). Some of the more alarming remedies have included the dried flesh of weasel, the blood of convicted criminals, and the testicles of beavers. One of the less obnoxious prescriptions was mistletoe, which, because it grows on oaks, which never fall, was thought to be good for the falling sickness!

The first drug which seems to have an undoubted effect on epilepsy was bromide, introduced by Locock in 1957. According to the account of Lennox, it appears that Locock had read of a German who had become impotent after taking bromide of potassium. Locock seems to have considered that epilepsy resulted from sexual excess, and he therefore used it for women with hysterical, and subsequently truly epileptic seizures. The idea that bromide dampens sexual desire remains. Soldiers in both World Wars were convinced that bromide was added to their tea to prevent sexuality interfering with fighting!

Bromide was undoubtedly successful. Aldren Turner, the father of my former colleague at St. Bartholomew's Hospital, attained a remission of seizures in 33 per cent of his patients, a record which is difficult to beat today, at least for those with established epilepsy. However, it had two main drawbacks. It caused a considerable depression in mental alertness, and unpleasant acne. It was recognized that the blood level of bromides could be used as an index of intoxication, although unfortunately there was no close relation between the blood level and the dose ingested, nor between the blood level and clinical effect. Much the same problems occur with the newer anticonvulsant drugs (see pages 94–5).

The first years of this century saw an enormous advance in synthetic organic chemistry. Veronal was synthesized in 1903, and phenobarbitone (Luminal) a few years later. Veronal was the first barbiturate sleeping drug, and phenobarbitone was first used in the treatment of epilepsy by Hauptmann in 1912. The drug rapidly entered routine use after the First World War, and remains in use today.

Many of the drugs now used have a similar molecular structure. The drug company, Park, Davis & Company provided a number of compounds to Putnam, an American neurologist in Boston. He and Merritt devised experiments whereby the protective effect of these could be assessed. Graduated electric shocks were used to induce seizures in cats, and the preventive effect of the compounds was measured. Many compounds were tried by Putnam and Merritt, and amongst the most successful and least toxic was phenytoin (Epanutin, Dilantin).

Following these discoveries, more and more drugs entered the field. Many have fallen by the wayside, largely because subsequent experience has not substantiated the first claims. Most neurologists confine their practice to the drugs listed in the top half of Table 7 (page 91), with some of their commoner trade names. Many unfamiliar tablets brought to me by patients from abroad turn out to have one or more of the well-recognized constituents, marketed under a name unfamiliar to us in Europe or the United States. The Grass Company has prepared an International Glossary of Anticonvulsant drugs, which I find invaluable.

The 'seven principles of anticonvulsant therapy' are shown in Table 4, and are now discussed.

1. Should anticonvulsants be given anyway?

Most neurologists will not advise anticonvulsant treatment after the first seizure. Only time will tell whether the seizure will remain isolated. Unfortunately some people do go on to have further seizures. In a report of young U.S. Navy personnel who had had one seizure, follow-up study showed that 49 of 77 (64 per cent) had a subsequent seizure within the next three years. If this experience is the rule, then 36 per cent of all those who had suffered a single seizure would be

Table 4. *The seven principles of anticonvulsant therapy*

---

1 Reconsider decision. Should anticonvulsants be given anyway?

2 Choose a drug, considering the following factors:
- The seizure type(s)
- Age
- The possibility of pregnancy
- Interaction with other drugs
- Price

3 Give only one drug, except in unusual circumstances.

4 Begin chosen drug in modest dosage.

5 Give full information to the patient about:
- The names and alternative names of the drug supplied
- The initial dosage schedule with dates of planned changes in dosage
- The need for compliance with instructions
- Adverse effects of the drugs

6 Monitor progress
- Inform subject of date and place of next review
- Monitor seizure frequency
- Monitor unwanted side effects of drugs
- Monitor blood level of drug

7 Determine policy for termination of treatment.

---

unnecessarily treated if anticonvulsants were routinely prescribed after the first attack. I do, however, consider giving anticonvulsants if the subject felt a further seizure could be disastrous to prospects of promotion in their career, or other prospects which they regard as important.

If seizures are very rare — separated by five or ten years without anticonvulsant medication, I would not think it worth the subject's while to take daily medication, unless, as in the case just mentioned, a further seizure might have a devastating affect on the subject's life. In both cases, the importance of driving may influence my advice. After a first seizure, English practice is to advise that the subject is ineligible to drive for one year (see page 137). Occasionally I see a patient who thinks that his employing company will stand for his not driving for one year, but might jib at a three-year ban, as would be necessary if he had a second seizure (but see pages 131–8 for a full discussion). In such circumstances I prescribe anticonvulsant medication after a single seizure.

There are people whose seizures can be clearly attributed in part to a non-recurring cause. For example, seizures may begin for the first time whilst the subject is on an antidepressant drug, such as amitriptyline, which is known to induce seizures in some people. Clearly the drug is not the only factor. Thousands of people take amitriptyline without having seizures. In those who do, the drug presumably acts on those with a low seizure threshold (see page 6). Nevertheless it would seem reasonable to see how such a person gets on without antidepressants, before prescribing anticonvulsants. Other precipitating factors, if specific, such as occur in epilepsy induced by television (see page 48) may be avoided, and obviate the need for anticonvulsants.

2. Choice of anticonvulsant drug and factors to be considered

The seizure type(s). The different types of seizure are reviewed on pages 13–22. As already explained, an accurate account both from the subject and any bystander is the most useful tool in categorizing a seizure, supplemented by the electroencephalogram.

There are horses for courses. Primidone, for example, is a moderately effective drug for grand mal and temporal lobe seizures, but is ineffective in petit mal absences.

Table 5 shows the anticonvulsant drugs which have been shown to be most effective in the various types of seizure. Many claims have been made for other drugs, and for the efficacy of these drugs in types of seizure other than those for which they are recommended in the Table. These claims often appeared to be substantial, but in the last decade clinicians and pharmacologists have become increasingly critical of claims resulting from inadequate assessment of

Table 5

Seizure type	Anticonvulsant drugs of choice	Therapeutic levels in serum (micromoles/litre)†	Typical adult dose per day (mg)
Typical abscences (petit mal)	sodium valproate	350–700	1 500
	ethosuximide	285–850	1 000
	clonazepam		
Myoclonic and akinetic seizures	sodium valproate	350–700	1 800
	nitrazepam		
	clonazepam		
Tonic-clonic seizures (grand mal) in association with typical abscences (petit mal)	sodium valproate	350–700	1 800
	phenytoin	28–100	300
	phenobarbitone	65–170	90
Tonic-clonic seizures (grand mal) in association with partial seizures, or partial seizures alone	carbamazepine	13–51	600
	phenytoin	40–100	300
	phenobarbitone	65–170	90
	primidone		750
Infantile spasms	ACTH		
	nitrazepam		

†The level below which therapeutic effects are unlikely to occur, and above which toxic effects are likely to occur.

86

Treatment

drugs. Dr. Alan Richens, in his book *Drug treatment of epilepsy* (Kimpton, London 1975) devotes a whole chapter to the proper design of a clinical trial of a new anticonvulsant. Many inadequate trials of anticonvulsant drugs have been carried out on groups of patients with epilepsy due to different causes, with different types of epileptic seizure, occurring with differing frequency. The patients are usually already on various other anticonvulsant drugs to which they have not responded, and which may interact in a complex way with the drug under trial. Finally there is often no clearly thought out method of assessing the results. It is probably meaningless to compare a reduction in the frequency of seizures amongst patients with so many variables. The best assessment — complete abolition of seizures — depends on a long follow-up study of many years, for the passage of which most doctors are too impatient to wait before publishing their results. It is not surprising that much mis-information has been published about anticonvulsant therapy based upon such muddled trials of drugs. Table 5 lists the types of seizure and the drugs which appear, from a distillation of all trials, to be most effective.

Age. Phenobarbitone causes unwanted effects in different age groups. Young children may become irritable, aggressive, and hyperactive. The middle-aged may complain bitterly of the sedative effect, whilst the elderly may become frankly confused. These are the principal reasons why phenobarbitone is now looked upon with less favour, although it is an extremely effective anticonvulsant. It should certainly be avoided in youth and old age if possible.

Schoolchildren naturally dislike having to take tablets at lunch-time whilst at school, as this draws unwanted attention. It may therefore be best to consider one of the drugs, such as phenytoin, that can be given in once daily dosage (see page 92).

Phenytoin, ethosuximide, and clonazepam are all available in liquid form, which may suit little children better than tablets or capsules.

87

Epilepsy: the facts

The possibility of pregnancy occurring during treatment. The drawbacks to giving anticonvulsants during pregnancy are discussed on pages 97–8.

Interaction with other drugs. The most frequent of such interactions is with the contraceptive pill. Some anticonvulsant drugs, notably phenytoin, phenobarbitone, primidone, and carbamazepine cause an increase in production of those enzymes in the liver which are responsible for the metabolism of a number of different compounds, including the drugs themselves. Enzyme induction of this type will lead to a more rapid breakdown of the steroid hormone oestrogen contained in the pill. Women with epilepsy must realize that their contraceptive protection may therefore be inadequate, particularly if using a low-oestrogen pill.

Anticonvulsant drugs will also enhance the metabolism of anticoagulant drugs, used in the treatment of venous thrombosis, and occasionally for those with other types of vascular disease. If given anticonvulsants, then such patients will need an increase in their anticoagulant dosage. The efficacy of phenylbutazone, used in the treatment of rheumatoid arthritis, of digitoxin, used in cardiac disease, and of the antidepressant drug nortriptyline are all reduced by anticonvulsant therapy. Conversely there are other drugs such as isoniazid, used in the treatment of tuberculosis, which may inhibit the breakdown of anticonvulsants, precipitating phenytoin intoxication if added to the medication of a patient well established on this drug. The antibiotic chloramphenicol, and disulfiram, used in the treatment of those with chronic alcoholism, may produce similar though less dramatic results.

Price. Fortunately none of the anticonvulsant drugs is expensive. Table 6 shows the cost of treating a subject for a year with the principal drugs. Readers with epilepsy in Great Britain should know that they are exempt from prescription charges. Application should be made on Form FPC91,

Treatment

Table 6. *Cost† of treating epilepsy for one year with different drugs*

Drug	Typical dosage		Cost (£)
phenobarbitone	90 mg/day		0.50
phenytoin	300 mg/day	(tablets)	2.96
		(capsules)	10.00
primidone	750 mg/day		7.31
carbamazepine	600 mg/day		48.30
sodium valproate	1 500 mg/day	(500 mg tablets)	160.000

†based on costs to hospital pharmacy — July 1980.

obtainable from any office of the Department of Health and Social Security.

3. Give only one drug, except in unusual circumstances

Just as there are interactions between anticonvulsant drugs and those drugs used for other conditions, so there are interactions between anticonvulsant drugs. Sulthiame (Ospolot) for example inhibits the metabolism of phenytoin and, to a lesser extent, that of phenobarbitone and primidone, after about an interval of two weeks. This is not just a theoretical problem, as a previously stable serum phenytoin may be elevated to toxic levels by the misguided addition of sulthiame. Indeed, if the serum phenytoin level before sulthiame is added is over 50 micromoles per litre (see page 86), intoxication is almost certain. Another example of interaction between anticonvulsants is the effect of carbamazepine on phenytoin, the serum level of which falls if carbamazepine is added to the regime.

Apart from these cogent biochemical reasons for avoiding polypharmacy, there are other reasons. First, it is rather depressing for the subject to feel that his epilepsy is so bad that he has to take 'all these drugs' — he may feel that the number of drugs prescribed is a direct indication of the

89

severity and difficulty of his epilepsy. Secondly, there is a very real risk of confusion between tablets, a problem avoided if only one drug is prescribed. Thirdly, it seems that the unwanted sedative effect of a combination of anticonvulsant drugs may be more than the sum, in so far as it can be estimated, of each drug separately.

4. Begin chosen drug in modest dosage

If a steady unchanging dose of anticonvulsant drug is given during the early weeks of treatment, it will take up to two weeks before the fluid spaces within and between the body's cells are saturated, and before metabolism settles down to a steady level at which the excretion and breakdown of the drug matches the daily intake. For the first two weeks, therefore, the serum level is rising slowly, and the subject's brain has a chance to become acclimatized to the change in its biochemical environment. Even so, however, it is often wise to begin with a dose less than the expected maintenance dose. The starting dose of primidone it usually about one-fifth of the final amount expected to be suitable for maintenance. Otherwise severe sedation may occur, and the subject will reject the drug without further trial.

5. Information to be given to the subject

The names and alternative names of the drug supplied. The doctor prescribing the chosen anticonvulsant drug should write the prescription in such a way that the chemist is instructed to label the container with the full name and strength of tablet of the drug. This is becoming increasingly common. There seems no reason in this day and age for potent drugs to be concealed in little brown bottles bearing the inscription such as 'The Tablets — to be taken as directed'. The subject should also know both the official name of the drug, and the alternative proprietary (trade) names that he might encounter. Some of the alternative names of the commonly prescribed drugs are shown in Table 7.

The initial dosage schedule, with dates of the planned changes in dosage. The strength in milligrams of the tablet or capsule dispensed, or the concentration of syrup or suspension, the

Table 7. *Anticonvulsant drugs in common use*

Official name	Trade names commonly encountered	Preparation
Drugs in common use		
phenytoin	Epanutin, Dilantin	tablets 25, 50, 100 mg capsules 50, 100 mg suspension 30 mg/ 5 ml
carbamazepine	Tegretol	tablets 100, 200 mg syrup 100 mg/5 ml
ethosuximide	Zarontin, Emeside	capsules 250 mg syrup 250 mg/5 ml
sodium valproate	Epilim, Depakin	tablets 200, 500 mg
phenobarbitone	Luminal	tablets 15, 30, 60 mg capsules 100 mg
nitrazepam	Mogadon	tablets 5, 10 mg
Drugs in less common use		
clonazepam	Rivotril	tablets 0.5, 2 mg syrup in some countries
diazepam	Valium	tablets 2, 5, 10 mg
primidone	Mysoline	tablets 250 mg
Drugs now rarely used		
acetazolamide	Diamox	tablets 250 mg
methyl pheno- barbitone	Prominal	tablets 30, 60, 200 mg
sulthiame	Ospolot	tablets 50, 200 mg
troxidone	Tridione	capsules 300 mg

times at which the drug should be taken, and the total daily dose in milligrams at commencement of therapy should all be written down. The doctor should also write down, with dates, any subsequent increases in dosage he wishes the patient to take before the next review. It is absolutely hopeless to expect anyone to remember instructions such as 'Take one of the small, unscored white tablets for ten days on going to bed, then take one of the small, unscored white tablets after breakfast with one of the larger, scored white tablets on going to bed for ten days, and then one of the larger, scored white tablets after breakfast and another one after dinner for ten days, and then one of the larger, scored white tablets three times a day after meals'. This would be a reasonable way of beginning therapy with carbamazepine, but all subjects would feel more confident with written instructions as shown in Table 8.

The need for compliance with instructions. The regularity with which the subject takes his medication is technically known as compliance — the patient is complying with his doctor's suggestions. Compliance is also a word used in engineering. Its reciprocal or opposite is resistance. The compliance of those taking anticonvulsant medication is likely to be higher, their resistance less, and the control of their seizures better, if they know what they are supposed to be doing.

The principle of anticonvulsant therapy is to maintain as steady as possible the level of anticonvulsant in their bodies, in order to elevate the threshold of seizures. Although doctors should make it clear that omitting doses may precipitate seizures, subjects should be reassured that omission of one or two doses of a slowly metabolized drug such as phenobarbitone or ethosuximide is unlikely to affect significantly the serum level. Even if phenobarbitone is stopped abruptly, it is approximately 100 hours before the serum level falls to half its previous value. This so-called 'half-life' is not the same for each drug. The half-life of ethosuximide is

Treatment

Table 8. *Example of a dosage schedule*

John Smith. Age 29.

Commencement of therapy on 13 February, 1981, with carbamazepine (Tegretol).

70 tablets of 200 mg dispensed; for 100 mg, divide a tablet.

Date	Dose (mg)	Time	Total daily dose (mg)
13–22 February	100	At bedtime	100
23 February–3 March	100 200	After breakfast At bedtime }	300
4–13 March	200 200	After breakfast At bedtime }	400
14–23 March	200 200 200	After breakfast After mid-day meal At bedtime	600

Date of next review: 23 March at Puddletown Health Centre.

Telephone Puddletown 453 (Dr. Philip Brown) in case of any difficulties. Occasionally skin rashes and drowsiness occur on first taking this drug.

also long — about 80 hours, but for carbamazepine and for sodium valproate it is much shorter, of the order of 12 hours. The half-life of primidone is complex, in so far as the breakdown products of metabolism are themselves active anticonvulsants — phenobarbitone being one of them. Phenytoin, also one of the drugs to be slowly metabolized, cannot strictly speaking be said to have a half-life. The enzyme system which breaks up the molecule may become saturated, so that the metabolism will take place at two different rates depending on whether or not there is still some free enzyme available.

It it certainly worth knowing a little about rates of the metabolism of drugs. The fact that half-lives are measured in many hours means that 'clock watching' is not necessary. It does not make a ha'porth of difference whether a tablet of carbamazepine is taken at noon or at 1.00 p.m., as long as a dose is taken sometime around the middle of the day. The very slow metabolism of phenobarbitone, ethosuximide, and phenytoin mean that it is perfectly acceptable to take the drug once a day — not three times a day as is still at present conventional. Experience shows that a large proportion of mid-day doses of any drug are forgotten. In practice, linking tablet taking to teeth cleaning at night, or at night and morning, is logical for most anticonvulsants, and good for the teeth.

From what has been said so far, it might be believed that one only had to measure the serum level of any anticonvulsant to predict the response, and, if the level proved to be inadequate, to predict the increment in oral dose necessary to raise the serum concentration of the drug to a level known to be therapeutic. Such a policy would depend on the following knowledge and assumptions that:

1. There are serum anticonvulsant levels below which therapeutic effects do not occur, and above which no further benefit is achieved without toxicity.

This assumption is probably not true. For example there are many patients who seem to have their seizures controlled by serum levels below the limits shown in Table 5. The drug may indeed be doing some good at very low levels, as stopping the drug may be associated with return of seizures. The lower limits in Table 5 indicate only the level below which therapeutic effects are not *likely* to occur. It may also sometimes be worth 'pressing' a drug so that the serum levels enter a range in which many show toxicity. An occasional subject, for example, may get worthwhile control of seizures by phenytoin, without evidence of toxicity, with a serum concentration of 110 micromoles per litre, but not at 90 micromoles per litre.

Treatment

2. There is a reasonable lack of fluctuation of serum anti-convulsant concentration, so that the level measured does not depend critically on the interval between the last dose and taking the sample of blood.

This assumption is dependent upon the half-life of the drug. For practical purposes it does not matter when, within the last 24 hours, the last dose of phenobarbitone, phenytoin, or ethosuximide was taken. There are fairly sharp fluctuations in serum level in relation to time of dosage in the case of sodium valproate and carbamazepine, so the interval between last dose and measurement must be considered when assessing the efficacy of the measured level.

3. There is a proportionate relationship between serum anticonvulsant concentration and biological effect on the brain.

This is about the most vexing assumption of all. First of all, the fraction of the drug bound to serum protein may vary, so that the biological availability also varies. Secondly, although it has been shown that serum levels of anti-convulsant reflect the levels actually present in the brain, the biological effect of that brain concentration may be very variable – some subjects showing clinical evidence of toxicity at levels which would be considered as 'normal' for the majority. Furthermore, there are now considerable doubts about equating biological efficacy of the various drugs against seizures with serum level in the case of two of the principal drugs – phenobarbitone and sodium valproate. In the case of phenobarbitone the receptors on the brain cells which interact with phenobarbitone change their characteristics so that 'tolerance' to the drug develops. This is clearly so in the case of the sedative effect of phenobarbitone, and may also be true of the anticonvulsant effect. In the case of valproate, the anticonvulsant effect may continue for some weeks after the drug is stopped. This may mean that the drug is bound to some intra-cellular structure, still exerting its anticonvulsant effect, long after it is undetectable in the blood.

Adverse effects of the drugs. Considering the length of time for which so many people receive anticonvulsant drugs, adverse effects are fortunately few. Adverse effects can be divided into those due to excessive dosage of the drug, those due to unwanted side-effects of the drug, and those reactions which a very few subjects experience due to an idiosyncratic reaction between the drug and their particular body chemistry.

Overdosage of phenobarbitone, phenytoin, and primidone all produce unsteadiness of gait, tremor of the hands, and slurring of speech, not necessarily with sedation. The symptoms are most pronounced in the case of phenytoin intoxication; they are similar to those of alcohol intoxication. Almost invariably the symptoms are reversible within a few days of omitting the drug or reducing the dosage. The neurologist will have little difficulty diagnosing the early stages of intoxication, but his judgement can be supported by an estimation of the serum anticonvulsant level.

There are a number of interesting unwanted side-effects of the drug. First amongst these is sedation. The ideal anticonvulsant drug would have solely an anti-epileptic effect, but some drugs also produce a mild degree of sedation — not necessarily drowsiness, but a perception by the subject that he is not functioning as well as he might. This effect is most pronounced in the case of the barbiturate drugs such as phenobarbitone. Research studies on volunteers undertaking various intellectual tasks have shown impairment of performance whilst taking phenobarbitone compared to their performance whilst taking a dummy tablet. Unwanted sedation is the principal reason for avoiding phenobarbitone and primidone. If it is necessary to use these drugs, then sedation is minimized if medication is begun in small dosage.

Although adults are often sedated by phenobarbitone, young children may become hyper-active and aggressive whilst on this drug, and old people often become confused. It should thus be avoided in these age groups.

Phenytoin has an unfortunate effect on the gums, which

tend to hypertrophy and grow down between the teeth. This can usually be kept at bay by twice daily brushing upwards and downwards with a medium bristle tooth brush. If necessary a dentist can push back the gums or remove the excessive tissue. This overgrowth of gum tissue is reflected in subtle changes in the lips and facial skin, which may become slightly 'fleshy'. Phenytoin and barbiturates predispose to acne of the face and back, and may cause some slight excess of facial hair. All these cosmetic effects may be a reason to avoid using these drugs in young people if possible. Sodium valproate, on the other hand, may cause hair to fall from the scalp in a small number of people. Regrowth of hair occurs on stopping the drug.

There are a number of other side-effects of anticonvulsant drugs. Phenobarbitone seems to affect the shoulder joint in a few people, so that it becomes stiff and painful. In others, changes in the tendons in the hands and connective tissue of the palms leads to a contracture (Dupuytren's contracture) of the hands. The increased production of liver enzymes caused by phenytoin (page 88) causes an excessive metabolism of the body's vitamin D supplies, which may lead to rickets, in the absence of adequate diet or sunlight (which helps form vitamin D).

Idiosyncratic effects of anticonvulsant drugs affect primarily the skin. If a skin rash other than acne appears within a few days of starting an anticonvulsant drug, then a change must be made. Occasionally the capacity of the bone marrow to form blood cells is affected.

The effects of anticonvulsant drugs on foetal development must also be considered. Since the thalidomide disaster, many women are anxious that any drug taken during pregnancy may harm the baby, and I am often asked whether I can be sure that a prospective mother will have a normal baby if she continues taking anticonvulsant drugs.

The first point to make is that no doctor can guarantee that any woman will have a completely normal baby. There is, unfortunately, a small proportion of malformed babies

Epilepsy: the facts

born to perfectly healthy mothers who have not taken any drugs at all during pregnancy. Many of these abnormalities are minor — a hare lip, or a web between two toes for example. Many such abnormalities are easily corrected by plastic surgery.

However, there is a slight increase in foetal abnormalities in the children of people with epilepsy. Analysis of large numbers of incidents suggests that drugs, particularly phenytoin and phenobarbitone, are playing a part. An epileptic woman taking both these drugs is between two or three times more likely to have an abnormal baby than other women, and perhaps eight times more likely to have a child with the specific abnormality of hare lip or cleft palate. The risk of congenital heart disease is increased by a factor of abour four. However, mothers must put these figures in perspective. In every 1 000 births in the general population — not those taking drugs — there will be about 2 cases of hare lip or cleft palate. Even if this average risk is increased eight-fold by drugs, 984 out of every 1 000 children born to epileptic mothers *won't* have these abnormalities.

The other side of the coin is that frequent grand mal seizures during pregnancy may harm the baby, either by direct injury to the abdomen as the mother falls, or by the seizure preventing a sufficient oxygenation of the mother's — and hence the baby's — blood. Both circumstances are exceptionally rare, but they may occur, and this is one reason why neurologists usually advise continuation of anticonvulsant drugs during pregnancy.

Any foetal damage due to drugs occurs in the first few weeks of pregnancy, perhaps even before the mother realizes that she is pregnant, and often before she books in for antenatal advice. Unless, therefore, the pregnancy is a planned one, the decision whether to stop drugs or not has, by default, been taken. It is already too late to influence foetal development, so the mother might as well continue anticonvulsant drugs, and protect the baby against the risk of her having a seizure.

Treatment

6. Monitor progress

The date and place of next review. No person with epilepsy beginning anticonvulsant therapy should be left in doubt as to whom he should turn if he runs into any trouble. In England this should always, in the first instance, be the general practitioner. It follows that there must be good communication between the neurologist, who may advise about treatment, and the family doctor, who should prescribe it and monitor progress. It is my view that the family doctor is in a far better position to look after the month-to-month management than the neurologist, who may be relatively inaccessible, working at a number of different hospitals with a changing group of registrars. Patients with epilepsy who come to neurological outpatient clinics for review every six months or so almost invariably end up seeing a different doctor on each occasion. The worst example that I found in our survey of epilepsy in Metropolitan London was the case of a woman who had attended a well-known hospital on 22 occasions. Inspection of the notes showed that she had seen 16 different doctors — but never the consultant nominally in charge of her case. Consultation with the neurologist should be reserved for when the family doctor wishes for advice about some particular aspect of management, or when seizures are clearly not being controlled by the policy first suggested by the neurologist.

Monitor seizure frequency. All patients should be encouraged to keep initially a record of the dates of their seizures, as without a record of the frequency of attacks, accurate assessment of the results of treatment is not practical. One has to admit, however, that careful records of very frequent partial seizures are not useful in the present state of knowledge, and a neurologist confronted with pages of carefully annotated events may feel overwhelmed by redundant information. Furthermore, it is not psychologically healthy for a young person to be kept constantly aware of his problems by careful documentation. He may spend hours poring over his charts in an attempt to discover some sort of pattern that will allow him to predict future seizures. I usually ask my patients to think through the past months and roughly assess the numbers of seizures on attendance for review. This seems to be a useful compromise. I always write down the date of the last seizure as it provides an anchor-point for recall at the next visit. Any seizure may prove to be the last, so some such record is necessary for the time when application for a driving licence is made (pages 131–8).

Monitor unwanted side-effects of drugs. These have already been listed on pages 96–8.

Monitor serum level of anticonvulsants. This is at present usually a hospital-based service, but it is to be hoped that family doctors will have direct access to the laboratory so that they can obtain estimates of serum anticonvulsant levels, and adjust the dosage to ensure that either seizure control is established, or at least a therapeutic serum level is achieved before a drug is abandoned and another chosen. With most drugs, serum levels are, in any one subject, roughly proportional to the oral dose. However, as explained on page 93, the enzyme system which metabolizes phenytoin may become saturated, so that a small increment in dose results in a very large, and potentially toxic rise in the serum phenytoin level.

7. Determine policy for termination of treatment

The prognosis of epilepsy is reviewed in the next chapter, but every person with epilepsy whose seizures appear to have been controlled by anticonvulsant drugs wants to know if he can safely stop the drugs without return of seizures. I find this one of the most difficult decisions in consultant practice. Most people whose seizures have stopped, view cessation of therapy as the final hallmark of cure – they still feel 'different' because they are taking tablets. Others are concerned about the possible long-term effects of medication, though trouble on this score is most unlikely.

Many of the published research papers on this point are inadequate. The same criticisms that I directed on page 87 at trials of anticonvulsant drugs apply. Relapse rates are reported in groups of people of different ages, with different types of seizure due to different causes beginning at different ages, treated for different periods with different anticonvulsants. From such studies — which are the best we have — the consensus is that it is reasonable to consider withdrawal of medication if a subject has been free from seizures for three years. I have to say, however, that the chances of a return of seizures within the next three years are about one in three for adults. Recurrence is most likely if seizures had been present for a long time before control was established, and if there is a structural brain abnormality present giving rise to partial seizures.

Many patients ask if they can have another EEG to see 'if it's safe to stop the drugs'. Unfortunately this has not proved a reliable guide, some subjects relapsing with a normal EEG, and others remaining free from seizures in spite of an abnormal record including paroxysmal activity.

There may well be factors which encourage a patient to continue drugs, rather than to try the effect of withdrawal. A trial of managing without therapy may be disastrous if it results in the loss of a driving licence only recently regained.

If the decision is made to withdraw medication, then present policy is to do this over a period of many months. There is good evidence that rapid withdrawal of barbiturates in non-epileptic addicts may precipitate seizures, so the policy of cautious withdrawal seems sensible. Unfortunately the occasional subject relapses shortly after the very last tablet was stopped, suggesting that his seizures were controlled by a tiny dose of anticonvulsants that would normally be considered inadequate for control of seizures.

More than any other decision in epilepsy, the decision to

101

stop medication must be a decision jointly negotiated between and made by the doctor and subject, the latter being fully aware of the possibility of relapse.

Treatment of infantile spasms

The treatment of this type of epilepsy is quite unlike any other — but then the syndrome is quite unlike any other epilepsy (see page 22). A characteristic EEG, of high voltage and grossly disorganized, is seen in this type of epilepsy, due to a variety of cerebral abnormalities found only early in life. In 1958 a beneficial effect of adrenocorticotrophic hormone was demonstrated. This is a hormone, made up of about 40 amino acids, which is secreted by the pituitary gland, and which stimulates the adrenal gland to release cortisone into the blood. Since then cortisone, or prednisone, a steroid related to cortisone, have also been shown to be effective.

The outcome of such treatment is still uncertain, but most paediatricians would begin with either ACTH or prednisone as soon as possible after diagnosis. Dosage is, by adult standards, very high — 40 units of ACTH a day for one or two weeks followed by 20 units a day for a longer period, or prednisone 2 milligrams per kilogram body weight a day. About half the children will respond well initially to such treatment but the longer-term prognosis for normal intellectual development and cessation of seizures is much less certain.

Status epilepticus

Occasionally seizures follow each other in rapid succession, without full recovery between each. As explained on page 26, grand mal status is a medical emergency. The lack of normal respiratory movements, in association with the extreme muscular contractions during the seizures, throw great stress on the cardiovascular system. Furthermore, the continuing lack of oxygen may cause brain damage. The principle of

Treatment

treatment is to terminate the seizures as rapidly as possible. The family doctor should first give an intravenous injection of diazepam — 10–15 mg for an adult. If this does not terminate the bout at once, admission to hospital will be necessary. There, the house physician will put up an intravenous infusion containing either diazepam, or another drug. Chlormethiazole and thiopentone are two commonly used alternatives. Suppression of seizures may require such considerable quantities of these drugs that normal respiration is suppressed also, so that the patient will require intensive nursing and possibly machine-assisted respiration. The object of the treatment is to induce a coma in which all abnormal electrical activity is suppressed for 24–48 hours. Although the EEG may be of some use in deciding when it is safe to reduce the dosage of the intravenous drug, the empirical decision is usually taken to lighten the drug-induced coma after about 36 hours. Obviously, when the status is terminated, a review of the usual oral anticonvulsant medication should be undertaken so that, as far as possible, a repetition is avoided.

The treatment of status epilepticus in which the seizures concerned are absence or complex partial seizures follows the same principles. As patients in such states may present only with a curious bewildered confusion, diagnosis may be delayed unless the previous history of epilepsy is known.

Modification of diet

The beneficial effects of fasting on seizures have been known for many years. In starvation, normal metabolism is altered with an increase of circulatory compounds known as ketones. Similar changes without starvation can be induced by the so called ketogenic diet, which is very rich in fat and oils, and relatively low in carbohydrate. This was introduced by Wilder at the Mayo Clinic in 1921. The classical ketogenic diet is so rich in fat as to be relatively unpalatable, and the constituents, such as cream, are expensive to buy. About ten

103

years ago, the policy of substituting triglyceride oils for part of the dietary fat made the diet cheaper and more palatable. The necessary oils have a molecule of medium length (compared to other oils) and are therefore known as medium-chain triglycerides (MCT). About 70 per cent of the total daily calorie is given as MCT oil, the remainder as protein and carbohydrate, with vitamin supplements. The advice of a skilled dietitian in preparing and monitoring the diet is obviously necessary. The drawbacks to the diet include the frequent occurrence of smelly diarrhoea, and occasional apparent reduction in rate of growth.

How this diet works is not known. The cell wall of neurones is made of lipids, so possibly there is some stabilizing effect of the diet on this membrane. However, there are secondary changes in the blood, such as a fall in serum alanine, an amino acid concerned with neurotransmitter synthesis, so the explanation of membrane-stabilization is probably too simplistic. In spite of all the fat and oil consumed there is no change in the serum cholesterol or in those fatty substances believed to be important factors causing coronary artery disease.

The trouble caused by the preparation of this diet, in addition to normal meals for other members of the family, and its relative unpalatability even with MCT oils, means that it is seldom used except in children with severe epilepsy refractory to anticonvulsants. Occasionally its use may be astonishingly successful, and the diet may merit more attention than has been given to it in recent years.

Surgery

Everyone is familiar with the broad division of the practice of medicine into medical and surgical methods of treatment. It is not surprising, therefore, that if epilepsy is poorly controlled by anticonvulsant drugs, the subject begins to believe that there might be the possibility of a radical surgical cure. The ideal of having 'something cut out', and being made as good as new appeals to us all.

Treatment

Surgical treatment depends upon two main ideas. The first is that a local epileptogenic lesion can be entirely excised, leaving behind only healthy brain. The second is that the spread of seizure discharge, as indicated roughly by the arrows in Figure 4 on page 14, can be interrupted by surgical division of fibre pathways.

The neurosurgeons Penfield, and later Rasmussen, in Montreal, were the first and principal practitioners of the first principle. By painstaking clinical and radiological work, EEG recordings, and finally by exploration of the surface of the brain under local anaesthesia, they identified and removed by careful suction abnormal areas of the cortex and subcortical white matter. Electrical recording from the surface of the brain at the time of operation is an essential adjunct to this approach, so that all electrically abnormal cortex is removed, if possible, even if it appears satisfactory on visual inspection. Of course, any such procedure must leave a scar on the brain, but it was hoped, and experience has proved, that a neat surgical scar is less epileptogenic than the original lesion, or the sort of scar caused by a head injury.

Although the Montreal workers published their results in exceptionally full and careful form, it is difficult to generalize from them to any particular new subject being considered for surgery. The anatomical extent and physiological behaviour of epileptogenic cortex is unique to the individual. Nevertheless, about two-thirds of carefully selected subjects are improved, and about one-third become seizure-free.

The next major development in the surgery of epilepsy was the concept that an epileptogenic lesion in the front part of the temporal lobe could be removed by amputating and discarding the lobe as a single block of tissue. This approach, pioneered by Falconer at the Maudsley Hospital in London, has the additional advantage of allowing careful microscopical assessment of the epileptogenic lesion which is presented to the pathologist as an intact specimen. Much has been learned about the causes of temporal lobe epilepsy by this procedure. About 40 per cent of subjects adequately selected for temporal lobectomy became free of seizures, and there is a reduction in seizure frequency in about another 40 per cent.

Surgical treatment is only able now to give such good results because the neurosurgeons, quite properly, refuse to consider subjects for operation unless they fulfil the criteria developed by experience over the last 40 years. The first criterion is obvious — that the subject should previously have tried adequate medical treatment. The introduction of measurement of serum levels of anticonvulsant drugs at least gives some objective measure of the extent to which drug treatment has been used. The second criterion is that of chronicity. No surgeon is going to consider a major operative procedure in the early years of epilepsy. Not only might the epilepsy remit spontaneously, but also a certain amount of time seems to be necessary for the development of epilepto-genic foci after damage to the cortex. The surgeon wants to be sure that there is only one focus of abnormal activity. Not only is there a practical limit to the bits of brain that he can remove, but experience has shown that temporal lobectomy on one side may cause a disastrous disturbance of memory if the other temporal lobe is also damaged. Serial EEG recordings over many months will be demanded so that the surgeon can be assured that all abnormal electrical activity has its structural origin in one temporal lobe. Probably no more than 30 people with epilepsy in the United Kingdom fulfil these criteria each year.

One interesting other benefit from temporal lobe surgery is improvement in behaviour and social functioning, which often seems disproportionately greater than which would be expected from control of seizures alone.

Very occasionally, more extensive surgical excisions are performed. Children with uncontrolled epilepsy in association with severe hemiplegia may benefit from better seizure control by removal of the greater part of the affected cerebral hemisphere. Unfortunately, intracranial haemorrhage into the cavity left may occur many years after operation, and this late complication has reduced enthusiasm for this procedure. It may remain, however, the only possibility of helping a child, and family, severely disabled by repeated seizures.

The other principle of surgical treatment depends upon interruption of fibre pathways by which epileptic discharges are propagated. This idea, attractive in theory, has proved disappointing in practice. Operations attempted have included division of the corpus callosum, that large band of fibres which transmits information from one hemisphere to another, and carefully placed surgical lesions in white matter close to the thalamus. Only a very few centres in the world are exploring such operations, which must, in the present state of knowledge, be regarded as a last resort.

Cerebellar stimulation

Another procedure which is being more actively explored is the effect of electrical stimulation on the cerebellum. This part of the brain, about the size of a small orange, lies below the cerebral hemispheres. Its principal identified function is to monitor and modify commands to contract muscles issuing from the cerebral cortex, so that the movement is smoothly and accurately executed. Loss of one half of the cerebellum results in loss of coordination of the limbs on the same side, and a tremor. All this seems far removed from epilepsy. However, the role of the cerebellum upon the cerebral cortex is basically inhibitory. It has been shown that not only does electrical stimulation of the cerebellum inhibit normal cortical neuronal activity, but experimental cortical seizure discharges as well. Cooper, in New York, has over the last eight years developed a technique whereby electrodes are placed on the inferior surface of the cerebellum, and activated at intervals by electromagnetic coupling through an antenna placed subcutaneously on the chest. Such treatment is clearly at an experimental stage, though rapidly moving out of it. The control of seizures in some patient has been striking.

Biofeedback

In the 1960s it became apparent that animals could be trained to modify bodily functions such as heart rate and blood pressure, which previously were not thought to be under 'voluntary' control. For example, continuous recordings of blood pressure can be made from the artery in the tail of a rat. Electronic circuitry can be designed so that the rat receives a weak electric shock every time the blood pressure exceeds a preset value. The rat, through this 'feedback' information, learns to control its blood pressure below this value.

A similar procedure has, in the last decade, been extended to 'controlling' the electroencephalogram, with a view to modifying seizure frequency. The basic mechanism is that the subjects with epilepsy are encouraged to increase certain 'normal' rhythms and to suppress epileptic activity in the EEG. It is quite easy to design circuitry so that a green light is visible to the subject if and only if his brain at that time is producing the chosen rhythm. The subject is asked to keep the green light on as much as possible, and there is no doubt that he can learn to modify his cerebral rhythms accordingly. The question of whether he can modify his seizure frequency is much less certain. Many of the published studies report fewer than five subjects, who have had training sessions once or twice weekly for up to a year. In these circumstances it is difficult to be sure that the reported partial control of seizures might not just be a capricious but transitory natural improvement in seizure frequency. Furthermore, some of the earlier studies did not adequately control for variations in anticonvulsant drug levels. Finally it is recognized that whatever the therapy under trial, the intensive interest shown in a subject's condition in an experimental situation may itself produce a placebo effect. Having said all this however, one recent study showed that 10 of 21 subjects with more than four major seizures a month, uncontrolled with anticonvulsants, did have a significant reduction in seizure frequency

Treatment

whilst receiving five one- or two-hour sessions of training per week for three to six weeks. Subjects have reported that, apart from a reduction in seizure frequency, biofeedback training decreases the severity of attacks, and allows them to 'think more clearly'. At this stage it must be said that EEG biofeedback is an unpredictable treatment which is extremely costly in terms of time and equipment used. However, further research in this field is fully justifiable.

6

Long term outlook

Many patients, family doctors, and even neurologists are remarkably pessimistic about the likelihood of seizures stopping — a pessimism which is unjustified by the facts. Pessimism stems from hospital experience. In the past, when neurologists were fewer on the ground, they tended to see only those with the worst epilepsy with the worst prognosis. As they taught the future general practitioners, these too were infected with the same pessimism.

What are the facts? The first point to define is what we mean by remission or cessation of seizures. Epilepsy was defined on page 6 as a 'continuing tendency to epileptic seizures'. A propensity to convulse, or a lower than average epileptic threshold, probably does continue throughout life as part of one's genetic inheritance. A man aged 30, who had some seizures in his teens, cannot be said to be entirely free from the risk of a further seizure until he is safely dead and buried — but his risk may have declined so that it has become, at the age of 30, only a little greater than that of the general population. Regardless of this philosophical discussion, what a person with epilepsy wants to know is whether, for all practical purposes, the seizures will stop. A remission, therefore, can be defined as a certain period free from seizures. Based on hospital practice, a number of studies have shown that there is only about a one-third chance of achieving a two-year period of freedom from seizures.

It was only in 1979 that an adequate study of the true rate of remission was published. Based on the survey from Minnesota already mentioned on page 43, neurologists and statisticians followed up all those residents of Olmstead County who had had more than one non-febrile seizure with

110

Long term outlook

onset between 1935 and 1974. Four hundred and fifty-seven subjects could be studied — 328 for more than 10 years and 141 for more than 20 years. Figure 13 is redrawn from this study. The ordinate (upright line on the graph) indicates the cumulative probability of achieving a remission of at least five years. It can be seen that, at one year after diagnosis, 42 per cent of the subjects had entered a seizure-free period that was to extend for at least five years. The net probability of being in remission currently (five years or more and continuing), was 61 per cent at 10 years after diagnosis and 70 per cent at 20 years after diagnosis. The difference between the top two curves represents the small numbers of patients who have one long remission of at least five years with subsequent relapse. The relapse rate in the first five years after achieving a remission of five years was 8 per cent. The bottom curve refers to those subjects in remission without drugs.

In summary, 20 years after the diagnosis of epilepsy, about 30 per cent of subjects continued to have seizures, 20 per cent continued to take anticonvulsant medication but had been free from seizures for at least five years, and about 50 per cent had been free from seizures without anticonvulsant medication for at least five years.

These are much more encouraging figures, but every person with epilepsy will want to know if he is going to be one of the lucky majority. Certain relevant factors can be identified. The first of these is the type of seizure. For example in this study, 70 per cent of those with absence seizures, without associated grand mal, were in remission 10 years after diagnosis, and 80 per cent 20 years after diagnosis. Furthermore, the younger the age at onset of this combination of seizure types, the more likely the chance of continuing remission. Conversely, the remission rates for those with complex partial (temporal lobe) seizures were substantially lower, and for those with neurological deficit dating from birth or infancy lower still — only about 46 per cent being in remission 20 years after onset.

It will be noted that the curves shown in Figure 13 flatten

111

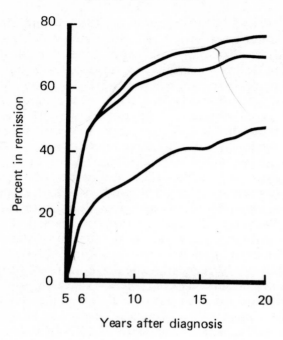

Fig. 13. Remission of epilepsy.
Top curve: probability of completing a period of five consecutive years without seizures. For example, six years after diagnosis 42 per cent of subjects have been seizure free for five years.
Middle curve: the probability of being in remission, at any time, for at least the past five years. The difference between the top and middle curve is due to relapse after achievement of a five-year remission. For example at 20 years after diagnosis 70 per cent are currently free from seizures and have been for five years and a further 6 per cent have had at least one seizure-free period of at least five years duration, but have subsequently relapsed.
Lowest curve: the probability of being free of seizures for at least five years whilst not taking anticonvulsant drugs.
In summary, 20 years after diagnosis 50 per cent have been free from seizures without anticonvulsants for at least five years. A further 20 per cent continue to take anticonvulsant medication and have also been free of seizures for at least five years. Seizures continue, in spite of medication, in 30 per cent.

off as time passes. This means that the probability of achieving remission, if it has not already been achieved, diminishes. For example, although the net probability of achieving remission within 10 years after diagnosis was 65 per cent, for patients not in remission five years after diagnosis, the probability of achieving remission within the next 10 years was only 33 per cent − the same proportion as based on the older surveys of established epilepsy based on hospital practice.

Many of the patients reported in this paper from the Mayo Clinic were studied, in part at least, before the advent of measurement of anticonvulsant levels and before the introduction of sodium valproate. It is likely therefore that, with modern management, we can be even more optimistic than these figures would suggest.

The study from the Mayo Clinic considered only a small number of children with epilepsy beginning in the first year of life, but in these children the prognosis is substantially worse. A recent series of papers from Paris has analysed the outcome of those whose seizures began between the ages of two months and one year. It should be remembered that the causes of such seizures, the age of onset, and the absence of associated fever places these infants in quite a different group from those children with febrile convulsions. Unfortunately it was found that more than half of such children were continuing to have seizures five years later. Particularly unfavourable factors were the presence of some associated intellectual deficit and neurological signs. Seventy-three per cent of such children were continuing to have seizures five years later, compared to 18 per cent of children with normal intellectual and physical development. It must be stressed that this report comes from a national paediatric centre, so it is likely that it is biased towards those with the worst problems.

Another long-term follow up study of children with epilepsy comes from Oxford. Two hundred children who had had at least one seizure in early childhood were assessed 25 years later. Two-thirds of the children had escaped any serious effects, but 10 per cent were found to have died, and about another 10 per cent were in some sort of institutional care. Even in those living in the community, continuing seizures were associated with greatly reduced educational and occupational achievement when compared to those whose epilepsy had ceased. As the authors point out, such a study goes a long way to justify parental anxiety of a child has a seizure. It should also encourage doctors to be vigorous in their efforts to terminate seizures as early as possible in life.

The prognosis of infantile spasms (salaam seizures) is particularly grave, not so much for cessation of seizures, which usually occurs, but for the later incidence of mental subnormality which, even with treatment, will be close to 80 per cent in an unselected group of children. There is, however, a sub-group with a much more favourable prognosis. This includes those children with previously normal development, those in whom no structural cause can be found, and those with spasms seemingly following pertussis (whooping-cough) immunization. One-third to one-half of these children recover completely.

7

Living with epilepsy—practical points

What to do during a seizure

What should a bystander do during a grand mal attack? The onset is often so sudden that it is difficult to do much at all in the early stages, though it may be possible to break the subject's fall. Parents or other relatives may recognize the warning signs that may occur if the generalized seizure is secondary to a focal discharge, and so may have time to help the subject to a chair or to a bed before the grand mal begins. It is usually possible to prevent injury occurring during an attack due, for example, to falling out of bed.

It is a great mistake, however, to try and open the subject's clenched mouth. The tongue, if bitten, is bitten at the onset of the attack, so there is no point in trying to save it. If the bystander uses his own fingers to try and force the mouth open, they may well be bitten in the clonic phase. If he tries to force a spoon or pencil between the teeth, the subject's teeth may be damaged. These manouvres are still sometimes attempted by tradition, and sometimes, presumably, because it is assumed that the subject's blue colour and arrest of breathing are due to obstruction to the passage of air into the lungs. Attempts to 'loosen the collar' presumably result from the same thoughts. However, all of us have enough gaps between our teeth to allow passage of air around them as the reader can readily show for himself by clenching his teeth, pinching his nose, and breathing in. Obstruction to the airway *may* occur during a seizure, if the subject is lying on his back. The tongue may then fall backwards into the pharynx, and, for this reason, it is worth turning someone suffering a grand mal seizure into a position halfway between

115

lying on his side and face, and thumping his back so that his tongue and any dentures that he may be wearing, fall forwards. This position also has the advantage that if the subject vomits, as occasionally happens, the contents of the stomach pass easily out of the mouth, and there is no danger of vomit entering the trachea and lungs.

If a grand mal seizure occurs in a public place, it usually happens that someone calls an ambulance − very often to the annoyance of the person with epilepsy, who is well on the way to recovery by the time the ambulance driver delivers him to the local hospital. There is no need to call an ambulance unless it is clear that repeated seizures are occurring.

There is usually little to be done during a partial seizure, except to stand by in a reassuring manner until seizure activity ceases. Occasionally gentle restraint may be necessary in the case of complex automatic behaviour (page 20).

Sensible restrictions on activities

Many relatives of people with epilepsy are naturally concerned as to what may happen during a seizure if they are not present to assist. I have known this anxiety carried to extremes. One of my patients, an epileptic woman of 30, was still sharing her parents' bedroom, as they were concerned that she might come to harm during a nocturnal seizure, even though she had had none for 15 years! In practice, harm resulting from seizures is exceptionally rare, but there are a few sensible precautions.

The first restriction − on driving − is more than sensible: it is a legal requirement. This is discussed in detail on pages 131–8. Sensible restrictions on employment are discussed on pages 126–7. We are here concerned with domestic and school life.

I do not believe that any one with frequent seizures should swim unless they are accompanied by an adult who both knows of their epilepsy, and is a sufficiently competent swimmer to bring an unconscious person safely ashore. Few people realize how difficult this is, so, if seizures are frequent it would be sensible to confine swimming to a pool, or, if in the sea, within wading distance of land.

Sailing is now very popular, and, as using a life-jacket is standard practice for all dinghy sailors, the risks are small. Skiing is acceptable to my mind, but not mountaineering, where the lives of others may depend upon continued concentration and performance. There is no reason to avoid team games, as there is no evidence that the rough and tumble of a football field precipitates seizures.

All children like to climb trees. At school they may be required to climb ropes in the gym. Those with frequent seizures should be discouraged from so doing.

I regard bicycle-riding in a suburban or rural environment as an acceptable risk. Obviously, as the density of traffic and frequency of seizures increases, so do the risks. Many people with epilepsy worry that they may come to harm while crossing a road. I have never had a patient to whom this has happened. Even during complex partial seizures it seems that sufficient awareness is retained to allow appropriate though unremembered decisions to be made.

At home, all fires must be guarded if someone with seizures is living in or visiting the house. The sort of guard required by law on gas and electric fires is adequate to prevent casual contact of the clothes or limbs of the healthy, but quite inadequate to protect against someone with epilepsy falling against it. A substantial purpose-built guard must be erected in front of the fire.

A mother with seizures should not bath her baby until her husband comes home. She may have a brief attack, and lose her hold on the baby. As an alternative, she can sponge her baby down on a napkin – a sort of 'blanket-bath'.

Unreasonable restrictions on activities

A healthy parent of a healthy child will encourage adventures, whilst taking sensible precautions to minimize serious risks, but there are always hazards in life — children without epilepsy can fall off their bicycles or into ponds. It is important that parents do not burden their children with epilepsy with unnecessary restrictions which limit social contact and development. Over-protection of the child will prevent the development of the sort of robust personality we all admire, even if we do not possess it ourselves.

Some families live in a constant fear of the recurrence of a seizure, so that tension pervades the house. Other parents are ashamed of their child's epilepsy. Children are quick to detect such attitudes, even if unspoken. They develop their personalities partly by reflection of the expectations of others. The epileptic child in such a family will grow up timid, embittered, and ashamed of his epilepsy, limiting his expectations and his chances in life.

Epilepsy as a social weapon

Families must be aware of ways in which epilepsy can be 'used'. The child or young person with epilepsy, knowing of his parents' anxiety about him, may manipulate them into granting him unreasonable requests. They may give in feeling sorry for his difficulties, or they may feel that they are avoiding an emotional upset that might precipitate a seizure. There is no reason why a child with epilepsy should not experience the same discipline as his siblings, who will become themselves jealous and unruly if they feel that one member of the family is being spoiled.

The other side of the coin is that parents may use the threat of epilepsy as a means of controlling behaviour which they otherwise cannot control. Examples I have met include limiting the hours of television watched, and the lateness of the hour by which an adolescent with epilepsy must return home.

Living with epilepsy – practical points

Prejudice, and telling others about epilepsy

It is unfortunately true that those with epilepsy do encounter a fair amount of prejudice against them, especially in the field of employment (page 127). This prejudice is perhaps based on dimly held knowledge of those in special care with the very worst epilepsy, often in association with mental retardation due to major neurological disease.

Prejudice against those with other illnesses is rare. No one minds if you have only one kidney, or varicose veins. Most people go out of their way to help a blind person, or someone in a wheel-chair. However, a blind or physically disabled person is immediately perceived as 'different'. Bystanders can make judgements about his abilities. They may relate to him in a special way – a manner which is instantly perceived and resented by an occupant of the wheelchair! Such a visible handicap is perceived and managed as such by society. Someone with epilepsy, however, is perfectly normal for 99.9 per cent of the time. His handicap is invisible. He then discredits himself, as it were, by having a seizure. His acquaintances feel deceived. The man who they thought was a bank manager turns out to be really an 'epileptic', passing himself off as normal. Such an attitude is ridiculous, yet there is persistent evidence for it. Such prejudice will, I hope, gradually fade, as misconceptions about epilepsy are dispelled. However, it would be foolish to deny its existence at the present time.

A major problem that someone with epilepsy has to decide, therefore, is how much to tell, and to whom. For example, no mother wants to tell everyone that her son has epilepsy, but, if the boy is staying the night at the house of a friend, it is only sensible to let his friend's parents know that he might have a seizure, and to tell them how to cope. Most parents would agree with this policy if the boy was having seizures every fortnight or so – but what if they occurred only every six months? Parents might feel that they were spoiling the boy's chances of friendship and social development if they sent him off with the label of epilepsy around his neck.

119

Epilepsy: the facts

Young people with epilepsy forming friendships with the opposite sex also suffer agonies about these decisions. If the epilepsy is not talked about early in the relationship the subject becomes more and more difficult to bring up. The problem may then be revealed by the occurrence of a seizure without prior explanation. Both parties feel devastated — the one guilty and ashamed at not having had the courage to explain the problem, the other surprised and ashamed of his surprise and inability to cope both with the seizure and his own feelings about it.

On balance, I am sure that it is best for a person with epilepsy to tell those he meets frequently something of the facts, so that they can cope in the presence of a seizure. Friends will appreciate the confidence shown in them by the fact of this disclosure.

As an entirely separate issue, a person with epilepsy may wish to carry in their handbag or wallet a card giving information about epilepsy, and the drugs that they are receiving. If, for example, a man is in a public place confused after a fit, such identification will avoid any misconceptions about the cause of the confusion. An excellent and elegant way of carrying this information is to wear a Medic Alert bracelet. This is a metal bracelet carrying the word 'epilepsy' and a telephone number engraved on the reverse. On ringing the number, which is manned 24 hours a day, staff can provide medical information from a card index. Further information about Medic Alert bracelets can be obtained from: Medic-Alert Foundation, 9 Hanover Street, London W1R 9HF (Tel. 01 499 2261) in the UK or Medic-Alert Foundation, 1000 North Palm Street, P.O. Box 1009, Turlock, Ca 95380 (Tel. 209 632 2371) in the US.

Psychiatric disorders and epilepsy

A person with epilepsy has to cope with the effects of his seizures on his chances in life — which may well be reduced if seizures are frequent. Throughout all his epileptic life he has

Living with epilepsy — practical points

to act as his own public relations officer, deciding how much to tell and how much to conceal. His circle of friends and choice of mate may well be narrowed. His inability to hold a driving licence and limitations in employment reduce his earning power, social status, and long-term financial security. By avoidance of factors which he believes may precipitate seizures, social activities may be greatly reduced. It is not surprising, therefore, that people with epilepsy become anxious, or depressed, or resentful and irritable. It may be that the character of the psychological disturbance depends in part upon the subject's genetic constitution.

The age of onset of epilepsy influences the psychological effects suffered. A robust man of 45 in good previous health who develops epilepsy following a head injury has established his personality, social life, family, and employment before the injury. Although he may encounter problems with future employment, there is no change in how his friends and family perceive him and react to him. The late age of onset and the clear-cut cause of seizures allows this man and his family to take up the position that, although he may have a few blackouts he is not really 'an epileptic'.

It is quite different for a girl whose epilepsy begins at the age of 12, with frequent seizures throughout her school career. Whatever her abilities, her friends and teachers perceive her as 'an epileptic'. Epilepsy dominates social intercourse, the development of personality, and possibilities of future employment and establishment of married life. Such a person will have more profound psychological difficulties than the 45-year-old man described above. Anxiety, depression, and resentment are entirely comprehensible reactions to the fact of epilepsy. One might say: 'I would feel like that if I had his problems'. To that extent, therefore, it would be wrong to categorize these psychological effects as an illness, though that does not mean that advice and support from friends, or the family doctor, or a psychiatrist may not aid the person with epilepsy to come to terms with his disability. However skilled the counsellor, however, I am convinced that

121

the ability to cope depends primarily upon the strength of personality of the person with epilepsy.

Occasionally depression in association with epilepsy may become so severe that treatment with an antidepressant drug is indicated. For reasons discussed on page 47, this drug should be chosen with care.

Depression and inability to cope with the life situation caused by epilepsy may be so severe as to cause the unfortunate sufferer to take his own life. Suicide is approximately five times commoner in those with epilepsy than in the general population.

A psychotic illness with symptoms similar to those of paranoid schizophrenia may occasionally be seen in those with epilepsy arising from a temporal lobe lesion. The occurrence of the psychosis is not necessarily related to the frequency of seizures. Indeed, there is a curious group of patients in whom the psychosis becomes prominent as seizures settle, only to remit as seizures return.

One cause of epilepsy is brain damage occurring at or around the time of birth (page 37). Children with such brain damage may be less intelligent than their siblings, be more easily distracted from work and play, and prone to emotional extremes. Because of constant restlessness, this behaviour is sometimes known as the 'hyperkinetic syndrome'. It should be understood that both the behaviour and the epilepsy share a common cause; the epilepsy in itself does not cause this behaviour.

Problems for women with epilepsy

These have been referred to at various places within the book. The effect of menstruation on seizure frequency is discussed on page 45. The interaction between anticonvulsant drugs and oral contraceptives is discussed on page 88. The effects of anticonvulsant drugs on the foetus are discussed on pages 97–8.

There remains to be discussed pregnancy and breast-feeding in relation to epilepsy.

Living with epilepsy — practical points

Some mothers report that their seizures become more frequent, others less frequent during pregnancy, and others have seizures which remain more or less unchanged in pregnancy. There seems no way of predicting what is going to happen in the first pregnancy, except that those with very frequent seizures are, unfortunately, likely to get worse. By and large, subsequent pregnancies in any one mother follow much the same pattern. An unexpected and totally unexplained finding has been that those pregnant with a male baby are rather more likely to have more frequent seizures. Although epilepsy may start for the first time during pregnancy, this usually seems to be coincidental, and there is no good evidence that pregnancy itself is a particularly potent event in *inducing* seizures.

One possible reason for an increase in frequency of seizures during pregnancy is that the metabolism of anticonvulsant drugs is changed. Such interactions between pregnancy and drug metabolism may be complex. Phenytoin, for example, is present in the blood in two fractions, one bound to plasma proteins, and one free. It is the free fraction that exerts the anticonvulsant effect. In pregnancy the total protein bound fraction may be reduced, but the free fraction remains unchanged. Estimating the total serum phenytoin in pregnancy may, therefore, give the false impression that anticonvulsant activity is less.

As a problem quite separate from epilepsy, convulsive seizures due to a complication of pregnancy — eclampsia — may occur in the later stages of pregnancy. In this complication, a sudden marked elevation of blood pressure produces changes in the blood vessels in the brain, resulting in generalized seizures. There is no relation between these seizures and continuing epilepsy. It is to avoid this complication — now fortunately rare in Great Britain — that obstetricians insist on taking the blood pressure at every antenatal visit, and advise increased rest if even a moderate elevation is noted.

Some anticonvulsant drugs pass the placenta into the

123

foetus. Phenobarbitone is perhaps the best-known example. After delivery the baby's serum phenobarbitone falls, and during this time he may be much more fractious and irritable than most new-born babies.

Many mothers on anticonvulsant drugs wonder whether they can breast-feed their babies. Careful studies have been made on this point, and only small quantities of the drugs are secreted into milk, so it is quite safe to breast-feed.

Sexual activity and epilepsy

Orgasm in both male and female is presumably accompanied by some sort of 'paroxysmal discharge of cerebral neurones'. This, and the impossibility of control of orgasm beyond a certain point, suggests an analogy with seizures. In fact seizures during or immediately after intercourse are exceptionally uncommon. When they do occur, they probably represent one of the types of reflex epilepsy described on page 48. Except in these rare cases, there is certainly no reason for avoiding intercourse on the grounds that seizures may be provoked.

Unfortunately epilepsy is sometimes accompanied by a decline in sexuality. Many adolescents find their initial dates worrying enough ('Which cinema should I take her too?' 'Should I let him kiss me?'), but how much more worrying must it be to take a girl out knowing that there is a chance, albeit a remote chance, that a seizure will occur during the date? Anxiety about contact with the opposite sex may have its basis in such entirely understandable problems of adolescence. However, there is evidence that a decline in sexuality may occur more frequently in those with seizures arising in the temporal lobe than in other types of seizures. Rarely sexual performance may improve after temporal lobe surgery.

Sometimes patients may complain about loss of libido and sexual performance after beginning anticonvulsant drugs. This seems to happen most frequently after phenobarbitone and primidone, but it is difficult to be sure how much is due to the drugs, and how much to social and psychological factors. The popular myth about bromides has already been mentioned on page 82.

Education

The vast majority of children with epilepsy are educated at normal schools alongside their brothers and sisters. Even if seizures are rare, the head of the school and the form teacher should be informed that a seizure might occur in class. The teachers will then know what to expect and what to do, and they may usefully involve other children in the care of the affected child during the seizure. There is no school activity which a child with epilepsy should not do on account of his seizures, with the exception of climbing ropes in the gym.

If the child has frequent seizures at school, which do not respond to anticonvulsant drugs, then there is a case for considering placement at one of the few special schools for children with epilepsy. Perhaps the best known of these is at Lingfield, Surrey, where about 300 children with epilepsy live in small family units and receive an excellent education planned according to their intellectual possibilities. In such an environment, seizures are of course every day events, and managed with a minimum of fuss. Any child demoralized and disturbed by frequent seizures at a normal school, often rejected by his schoolmates as a playmate, may benefit enormously by transfer to such a school.

Another benefit that may be gained by transfer to a residential school such as Lingfield is separation from the family. Mothers and fathers may naturally find this hard to believe, but through their natural concern for their child with epilepsy, they may overprotect him from normal social activities and development. Such a child may blossom unexpectedly in the atmosphere of a special school where everyone has the same problem, and some are even worse than he!

Arrangements for special schooling are made through the Education Authority in the territory of which the child lives.

It may be that a child with epilepsy, though not having frequent seizures, is doing badly in his school work. The first possibility to be considered is that he is having many more seizures — absence attacks or complex partial seizures — than are realized by him or his family. An observant schoolteacher may point this out. The second possibility is that his intellect and drive are dulled by an unnecessarily excessive dose of anti-convulsant drugs. The serum level should be checked. The third possibility — by far the most likely — is that the epilepsy and the intellectual difficulty share a common cause due to cerebral damage at birth or in early childhood. In these circum-stances a psychologist will assess the child's strengths and weak-nesses, and advise on the best type of schooling for his abilities.

By and large, schooling for children with epilepsy does not present too much of a problem. Until school leaving-age he is placed, in the United Kingdom without charge, in an environ-ment which occupies him in a structured manner for about three quarters of the year. At the age of 16 he then has to find himself a job. This is when the crunch comes.

Employment

It is not sensible to be a steeple-jack or scaffolder if one has many seizures. But just what restrictions on employment should be applied to those with epilepsy?

First of all, there are the legal restrictions on driving, which are fully discussed on pages 131–8. An epileptic seizure after the age of three years prevents a person driving a Heavy Goods Vehicle. Epileptic seizures occurring subsequently may render the subject ineligible to hold an ordinary driving licence. This effectively stops employment as a travelling representa-tive, for example, but these regulations have a wider effect in making travel to a job more difficult, especially in rural areas, however suitable that job may be.

Living with epilepsy – practical points

Driving is the most obvious way in which a person with epilepsy can harm others, as well as himself, during a seizure. But there are occupations of heavy personal responsibility to others which those with uncontrolled seizures must not do. Surgery and nursing are obvious examples from my own profession. The occupations of airline pilot, and bus, train, mass transit and crane driver, railway signalman, and merchant navy sailor, are other examples. The Armed Forces and Police also exclude those with continuing seizures.

In other jobs, there is no real risk to innocent bystanders during a seizure, but there is a substantial risk of injury or death to the person with continuing epilepsy. The operation of heavy moving machinery, including agricultural machinery, work near conveyor belts, work at heights, particularly in the construction or electric power industries, and work underground or underwater should all be avoided. However keen the subject may be to take his own life in his hands, it is not fair to burden employers if there is a substantial risk of a mutilating or fatal accident.

One of the agonizing questions that someone with infrequent seizures must ask himself is whether to tell a potential employer about them. Obviously it is best if he does, because the employer can take into account any remote risks about which the applicant is unaware. The employer can make an occasional allowance for rare but expected absences from work, and he can, in an informed way, cope with occasional seizures at work. The truth of the matter is that many employers reject those with seizures which are few and far between, or those who have had no seizures for some years, for jobs which carry virtually no risk to the person with epilepsy or to others.

Surveys of public attitudes towards those with epilepsy are meaningless, insofar as potential employers may well make favourable remarks about the employment of a hypothetical person with epilepsy in response to an interviewer, because this is the polite and modern thing to say. However, it is his actual behaviour in hiring and firing that counts. A truer measure of the amount of prejudice against employing people with epilepsy would be to send round two personable young women with equal qualifications in response to 100 advertisements for a post as a secretary, for example. In half the interviews each applicant would indicate that they suffered from mild, well-controlled epilepsy. The success rate with and without revealing this information would be a fair guide to current prejudice against the employment of those with epilepsy. Unfortunately I am sure that such a study would be unethical, insofar as it would waste the time and resources of employers. Nevertheless, I would be fascinated to know the answer!

Those with epilepsy intuitively know the likely result from the results of their own interviews. Our survey of people with epilepsy in London showed that over half those who had had two or more full-time jobs after the onset of epilepsy had never disclosed their epilepsy to an employer, and only one in ten had *always* revealed it. Furthermore if seizures were infrequent or nocturnal, so that the applicant considered that he had a good chance of getting away with concealment, the employer was virtually never informed. Whilst not condoning or encouraging dishonesty, the practical success of this policy can be judged by the fact that 74 per cent of the men of employable age with epilepsy were employed, compared to 81 per cent of male workers of the same age group in the United Kingdom as a whole.

Whatever the policy about disclosure, an applicant for a job will be more successful if he follows the general rules of taking care with his written application, taking trouble to inform himself about the responsibilities of the post and about the employer, presenting himself well at interview, selling his own ability to do the job, and convincing the prospective employer that he has an enthusiastic desire to work. What is absolutely disastrous is for frequent rejections to lead to the development of a chip on the shoulder, so that a potential employer is confronted by the attitude 'I have epilepsy; you haven't; you have a duty to employ me'. I have had patients with rare seizures who succeed in presenting themselves and their epilepsy in such an unfavourable light that I feel there can be no strong motivation to obtain work.

Obtaining a job is obviously only the first step. Most of us want promotion up to the limits of our energies and capabilities, and here again epilepsy, even if well controlled, often spoils chances in life. It is difficult to measure the frequency with which those well qualified for promotion are overlooked, but we found that the rate of dismissal following the onset of epilepsy was increased approximately sixfold.

There is another more subtle way in which epilepsy can hinder employment and promotion. The fear of encountering rejection, or the fear of leaving an established position with a tolerant employer may cause the person with epilepsy to deny himself chances for betterment. Just as the employer may be prejudiced against 'epileptics' so may the epileptic be prejudiced against 'employers', believing them all to be lacking in understanding.

There may be an advantage in young people with epilepsy seeking a career in small organizations, where regulations for employment, sick leave, insurance and pensions are flexible compared to those of, for example, the Civil Service.

As might be expected, if seizures occur frequently, our study showed that it was much more difficult to hold down a job. A third of the unemployed were having generalized seizures monthly or more frequently, whilst only 2 per cent of the employed were suffering equivalently. Roughly the same proportions held true for partial seizures. Apart from seizure frequency, the main barrier to employment is lack of any special skill. Our survey found, as could have been foretold, that virtually all those with frequent seizures and no special skill were unemployed. It is here that specialist advice from employment agencies should be sought.

In the United Kingdom the Manpower Services Commission employs about 4000 advisers, of whom about 500 are specially trained in the needs of and abilities of people with various disabilities. These Disablement Resettlement Officers (DROs) will be happy to advise any person with any disability. Appointments can be made for an interview at any Employment Office or Job Centre. It is not necessary to be registered as disabled to use many of the services provided by the DRO, though they may recommend registration. All employers of more than 20 people have a statutory requirement in the United Kingdom, under the Disabled Persons (Employment) Acts of 1944 and 1958 to employ a quota of 3 per cent of their employees from those on the Disabled Register. Consequently a big firm is keen to employ someone capable of good work if they happen to be on the Register. Before registration, the general practitioner or neurologist will, with the subject's consent, fill in a special form which provides basic information about the type and frequency of seizures, and any other associated disability.

The DRO may consider that a person with epilepsy may benefit from a Training Opportunities Course, to equip him with a special skill not already possessed. For example, a nurse with frequent seizures might no longer be suitable for nursing, until the seizures were controlled, and the DRO might well advise that she take a secretarial course. This could be done at the expense of the Manpower Services Commission, which also pays a tax-free maintenance allowance during the course, and maintains National Insurance contributions.

For those with very frequent seizures, possibly in association with mental retardation due to birth or other injury, the DRO may advise a job in 'sheltered' employment, in which severely handicapped people work under supervision in conditions which are an approximation to a light job. In the United Kingdom there are about 1000 people with epilepsy in industrial workshops in such sheltered employment. Local authorities are encouraged to employ people with epilepsy in their parks and gardens, as the authority is assisted through the sheltered employment grant scheme.

The DRO can also help by advising about the Mobility

Living with epilepsy – practical points

Allowance, a tax-free grant to those unable to manage public transport. He may also be able to authorize the free loan of certain equipment to allow people to cope with a job they would otherwise be unable to do. He may also authorize payments of grants to employers, both towards the cost of necessary adaptations to enable the employment of specific disabled employees, and to encourage an introductory trial period of a specific disabled employee. Finally, in rare instances, a disabled person may be given a grant to help set up a small business that he can run on his own account, usually at home.

There will always be a nucleus of people with epilepsy who are unemployed, either temporarily or more or less permanently. The person who is capable of work but unemployed may, as time passes, become progressively more unemployable if not given occupation and support. It is here that local authority social workers and epilepsy Associations can help.

Driving and epilepsy

There are few aspects of having epilepsy in adult life that cause greater distress than the necessary legal restrictions on driving. For some people owning and using a car is a hobby in itself – albeit an expensive one. Others, particularly those living in rural areas where public transport is limited or non-existent find car ownership and driving almost necessary for shopping and social contact, and for getting to work. For some people, such as sales representatives, driving a car is an essential part of their work. Finally there are jobs such as delivery van driver in which driving is the sole function of employment, and any restriction on driving will cause the employee to lose his job.

Eligibility to hold a driving licence in Great Britain is determined by the Motor Vehicles (Driving Licences) Regulations 1971. Section 20 refers specifically to the problem of epilepsy. The Regulations in the relevant paragraph (20, 2) read in full:

Epilepsy: the facts

Epilepsy is prescribed for the purpose of section 100 (3) (b) of the Act of 1960 and an applicant for a licence suffering from epilepsy shall satisfy the conditions that —
(a) he shall have been free from any epileptic attack whilst awake for at least three years from the date when the licence is to have effect;
(b) in the case of an applicant who has had such attacks whilst asleep during that period he shall have been subject to such attacks whilst asleep but not whilst awake since before the beginning of that period;
(c) the driving of a vehicle by him in pursuance of the licence is not likely to be a source of danger to the public.

These Regulations are, I believe, a reasonable attempt to protect the public from the chances of meeting a driver who is briefly incapable of controlling his car because of a seizure. The Regulations are also fair to those with epilepsy insofar as they clearly state the circumstances under which they can drive.

What actually happens in practice? Take the example of a man who has held a licence for several years, and then has two grand mal seizures at work within a month. His general practitioner or neurologist will explain that he is no longer eligible to hold a driving licence. It is not the responsibility of either doctor to inform the licensing authority of this, but the doctor will record in his notes the fact that he has explained the position to his patient. It is the driver's responsibility to take action. Inside each British Driving Licence is the statement 'You are required by law to inform DVLC Swansea SA99 1AT at once if you have any disability which is or may become likely to affect your fitness as a driver, unless you do not expect it to last for more than three months'. The patient should write a brief note to the Licensing Centre at Swansea (the address above being sufficient) explaining the details and enclosing the licence, which will be acknowledged. No further action is necessary.

If all goes well for this man, and he has no further seizures after the first two, he becomes eligible to hold a driving licence three years after the date of the last attack. He then completes an application form as usual. In Section 6d, or in a covering letter if there is insufficient space on the form, he writes briefly exactly what has occurred, refers to his earlier letter, states the date of his last seizure, and gives the name and address of his general practitioner or neurologist to whom reference can be made. After a short interval, he will receive his new licence.

All this seems entirely straightforward, but I know that many people with epilepsy find the Regulations hard to accept. Doctors will appreciate the difficulties that may be caused by giving up driving. Driving is usually an essential part of their work, so they do not have to make great leaps of imagination to realize the difficulties that a ban on driving may cause. Unfortunately the law does not take hardship into account. The doctor should, however, not only advise his patient of the law, but also, from his experience, advise the patient how to cope with his changed circumstances. He is in a position to influence decisions of employers about the nature of his patient's work. He can write to the employer, with his patient's consent, supporting a request for a change of job within the same company. In his letter he does not necessarily have to say that his patient has epilepsy, only that he is not able to drive for medical reasons, and is not likely to be able to drive for some years. Such letters may well influence company decisions. I have known many examples of this. A travelling salesman has become a successful office-bound sales manager, a busy surveyor has taken on increased training responsibilities, and a delivery van driver has been employed within the factory making the goods he was previously delivering. Obviously such changes are easier within large organizations with their greater variety of jobs, and probably easier in middle-class jobs in which there are less difficulties with different trades unions controlling different types of work.

I usually advise people living in rural areas not to move house just because of their new inability to drive. If it seems likely that the seizures can be easily controlled, then it is probably better to cope somehow for the time necessary, rather than disturb the whole family's way of life. The

133

person with epilepsy is the only one who can decide whether to move, but his doctor should give him sufficient information about the probability of seizure control to allow an informed decision.

Sometimes a person with epilepsy will say that he considers it safe to drive as he always gets a warning of his attacks. Leaving aside the legal point — that he is ineligible, and unfortunately his opinion does not count — I explain that his warning is the start of the cerebral events which form the early part of the seizure itself. The fact that to date the progression of the seizure discharge has been sufficiently slow to allow him to stop his car safely does not mean that this will always be the case. Such an epileptic may well have a sudden grand mal seizure without any warning.

Again, a person with epilepsy may indicate that he considers it safe for him to drive, as all his seizures are small ones — perhaps temporal lobe seizures in which consciousness is disturbed in only a minor way. I have to say that the law does not distinguish between the various types of seizures. I also have to say that his next seizure unfortunately may be a grand mal one, and that in any event catastrophe is as likely to be caused by a momentary lowering of consciousness as by a major fit.

With the exception of seizures which have always occurred during sleep, about which I write on page 135, the time of seizure is irrelevant. It is useless for the patient to say to his doctor that his seizures always occur in the evening, or sometimes even: 'I've never had one whilst driving', as the next seizure may well be when he is in the driving seat.

Sometimes a patient may feel that the events which have led him to the doctor are not epileptic in nature, and the proposed ban on driving in some way reinforces this view. All a doctor can do in such circumstances is to disagree, and advise that his patient seeks a further opinion. As noted above, it is not a doctor's responsibility to inform the licensing authority of his patient's epilepsy. It may be, however, that if he is convinced of the diagnosis, if he believes that there is

Living with epilepsy – practical points

a real risk to the public, and if the patient refuses to seek a further opinion, he may feel that his responsibility to the public at large over-rides his responsibility to his individual patient.

There are, however, circumstances in which the occurrence of epileptic seizures is not automatically associated with loss of eligibility to hold a driving licence. The Regulations quoted on page 132 state 'in the case of an applicant who has had such attacks whilst asleep during that period (of three years) he shall have been subject to such attacks whilst asleep but not whilst awake since before the beginning of that period'. There are some people, though not many, who only have fits during sleep; three years seems a reasonable period to allow one to see if that is the case. After that, even if attacks do occur in sleep and never whilst awake, a person can nevertheless drive.

The Regulations are careful to state 'attacks whilst asleep' rather than nocturnal attacks, to take account of those who are on night shift and sleep during the day. The concession to those who have only had attacks whilst asleep is in fact a generous one, insofar as a follow-up study by one neurologist of those who had only had nocturnal seizures showed that about one-third had a seizure whilst awake within the next five years. Of course a single seizure of any type whilst awake immediately renders the person who until then has only had seizures whilst asleep ineligible to drive. Likewise a single seizure whilst awake earlier in life prevents the application of this concession even if all subsequent seizures are whilst asleep.

The Regulations state nothing about anticonvulsant medication. The law is, as it were, interested in seizures and not in drugs. This means that there is no need to withdraw medication after a seizure-free interval so that the patient can resume driving. On common-sense grounds it is probably marginally safer to be a passenger with someone who has had seizures in the past, who remains on anticonvulsant drugs, rather than travel with someone who had his last seizure three years ago and stopped his drugs yesterday.

The graph shown on page 112 indicates that even if a remission of seizures lasting five years has occurred, relapses do unfortunately occur. The relapse rate in the first five years after achieving a remission of five years was 8 per cent. The Department of Transport in the United Kingdom has found that about a third of those who stop treatment on medical advice will have a further attack at some time, and of those about a half will have the recurrence within a year. Many will therefore consider it an additional safeguard to continue anticonvulsants, if driving, even if they are free from attacks.

Restrictions on those who wish to drive heavy goods vehicles are even more strict. The appropriate Regulations are the Heavy Goods Vehicles (Drivers' Licences) Regulations 1969 and (Amendment) Regulations 1971. The amended paragraph (4,b) reads:

(b) he shall not —
> (i) at any time since he attained the age of three years, have had an epileptic attack, or
> (ii) suffer from any disease or disability likely to cause the driving by him of a heavy goods vehicle to be a source of danger to the public.

These Regulations effectively bar any one from holding a HGV licence if they have had a seizure of any type after the age of three. It is probable that a febrile convulsion in a toddler of four might not be a ban to driving a heavy goods vehicle in later life, as this legitimately could be regarded as a non-epileptic attack.

Borderline cases of the type just mentioned are not uncommon in the much larger field of ordinary driving licences. For example, young adults who have successfully come through a few petit mal and grand mal attacks in childhood may have a few morning myoclonic jerks on rare occasions. Such patients often tell me that there is no detectable disturbance of their consciousness during such jerks. Many patients certainly do not regard such occasional jerks as fits, and yet, as they are the product of a paroxysmal discharge of brain cells, they are, technically, seizures. It is to help in advising on such borderline cases as this that the Department of Transport has available an Honorary Medical Advisory Panel on Epilepsy. It is open to any applicant for a licence who disagrees with the Department's refusal to grant him a licence, on the grounds that he has epilepsy and does not satisfy the requirements of the Regulations, to appeal to the Advisory Panel. From a compilation of the advice given by members of the Panel, a set of guidelines has been drawn up by the Medical Officers of the Department of Transport. If there is doubt in their minds, the matter is referred to the appropriate specialist, and I understand that that happens several times each week.

One question to be decided is the action to be taken after the first seizure. The problem, of course, is whether this seizure will remain a solitary one, or prove to be the fore-runner of others. The definition of epilepsy adopted in this book, discussed on page 6 is 'a continuing tendency to non-febrile epileptic seizures'. By this definition, a single seizure is insufficient to make the diagnosis of epilepsy. However, a follow-up study on naval personnel showed that about two-thirds of a group of young men developed a second seizure within three years of their first. It is therefore reasonable to demand a probationary period without driving after the first seizure. In view of the naval statistics quoted above, the practice of the Panel is generous to the applicant for a licence. A person with an isolated fit might well be allowed to drive after a year, though in exceptional circumstances this period might be reduced at the discretion of the Advisory Panel.

Finally, before leaving this vexed question of driving, I should add two further points. So far I have written exclus-ively about the practice in Great Britain. The requirements for eligibility vary from country to country, and, in the United States, from State to State. Enquiry must be made of the licensing authority in each country in which it is wished

137

to drive. Secondly, I am fully aware that many patients who are ineligible to drive do in fact do so. In our own survey of people with epilepsy in Greater London, 12 out of 62 currently ineligible to drive were in fact doing so. This is not always wilful recklessness. Only 3 of the 12 were both aware of the diagnosis, and admitted that they had been told not to drive. Some of the remainder did not realize, so they said, that they had epilepsy, or they felt that they had received explicit or implicit consent to their driving from their doctors.

Those who knowingly drive when ineligible must realize that their insurance policies would almost certainly be void if they had an accident. But the terrible risk of killing or maiming another innocent road user should be sufficient discouragement.

There are no restrictions — other than those of commonsense — on riding a pedal bicycle. Even if the rider has a seizure, he is likely to damage only himself.

Life insurance

One of the few ways that an average man has of building capital throughout his lifetime is by house purchase and by payments into regular saving schemes such as with-profits insurance policies — often by a combination of both. A married man will also usually wish to provide some sort of monetary support to his surviving spouse or children in the event of his unexpectedly early death. In short, life insurance is now regarded as part of nearly everyone's everyday financial arrangements.

Life Insurance companies are in business, in the final analysis, to provide a financial return for their shareholders, or, in the case of a Mutual Office to provide a fair deal for all policy-holders. It has to be admitted that the mortality of *all* those with seizures from *all* causes is higher than the general population. It is therefore not surprising that the Life Offices, if they accept the risk of underwriting the lives of those with epilepsy, require an excess premium to compensate them for the excess risk.

How is this excess premium calculated? The insurance industry uses statistics based on their past experience. As in employment (see page 128), it is probable that those with a few seizures calculate the risk of 'getting away with' concealment. In a financial transaction such as insurance, concealment of epilepsy is clearly fraudulent, and any policy arranged in this way is void. In so far as the statistical data of the Life Offices cannot reflect those with a few seizures who have concealed their epilepsy, it is probable that their experience of the mortality of those with declared epilepsy is worse than the true mortality. This experience tends to inflate the excess premium, but I believe that there are other factors. The Offices may be corporately possessed of some of the misconceptions about epilepsy that this book is trying to dispel. Although they employ a medical officer, few if any of these advisers are neurologists, and a single physician can hardly be expected to provide informed and modern statistics about the diseases suffered by each and every proposer. Furthermore the industry as a whole does not distinguish between different types of seizure occurring with different frequencies and due to different causes. In these circumstances the Offices adopt an attitude of 'better be safe than sorry' and charge a premium that is significantly in excess of standard rates.

There is often a considerable difference between the excess rates quoted by different Offices, so it is well worth while seeking professional advice from an insurance broker. In London, the firm of Tyser and Company, Corn Exchange Building, 52–57 Mark Lane, London EC3R 7SS have built up a considerable experience of arranging Life Insurance for those with epilepsy. In general they expect that any proposer with epilepsy should have been adequately investigated to exclude a progressive organic cause, and that the proposer should be reliable at taking his prescribed treatment and in following medical advice. It is very much easier to arrange insurance for those capable of employment and without intellectual impairment, although in other cases a quotation can usually be obtained.

I asked Tyser and Company for their views about three specific examples. Although useful as a general guide, readers must understand that rates will vary as each person with epilepsy is different both in his problems and in his requirements for insurance.

Proposal 1. A man aged 27 next birthday who had frequent seizures in childhood, several seizures in adolescence, and none over the last eight years.

Ordinary rates of premium would be allowed for this case, for any class of Assurance.

Proposal 2. A man aged 33 next birthday who had a single seizure one year ago. No evidence of any progressive organic disease.

For Term Assurance, where the ordinary rate of premium is very low, a loading of 50 per cent would be considered by some Offices. For other types of insurance the market would consider that a small loading for a short period of one or two years was justifiable. It might be possible to gain acceptance at normal rates, and this would be easier if the interval between the seizures and the proposal were longer.

Proposal 3. A man aged 25 next birthday who has had frequent grand mal fits since the age of 16, with four fits in the last year.

Assurable, but subject to an extra premium. The actual amount would probably vary among those Life Offices which are prepared to accept proposals from those with epilepsy, but in terms of additional mortality, one underwriter considers that plus 100 per cent would be a reasonable loading. At first sight this appears high, but regard should be given to the very low mortality rate of assured lives at this young age. In monetary terms the additional premium for Whole of Life Assurance would be £2.50 per annum for each £1000 of sum assured. One underwriter's practice would be to limit the term of payment of this extra premium to a period of ten years, but this is by no means general within the industry.

Special care for those with the worst epilepsy

Most people with frequent seizures are looked after at home by devoted parents or spouses. Sometimes a fragile situation breaks down and it is clear that a person with epilepsy cannot cope at home. Obviously if it is believed that this is a purely temporary set-back likely to be improved by modification of anticonvulsant drugs, then the family doctor will arrange a short stay in a neurological unit or in a special centre for epilepsy. Occasionally, however, it is obvious that neither the domestic situation of the person with epilepsy, nor his epilepsy, is going to improve in the foreseeable future, and long-stay care has to be arranged. The precipitating factor is very often the illness or death of the last surviving supporting relative.

In the middle of the last century, an increasing social committment to those less fortunate than the majority resulted in the establishment of 'colonies' for people with epilepsy. The general plan of such colonies in Europe was of a totally self-contained institution. During the day, the people with epilepsy would work in the open air, in arable and stock farming, and at night they would return to dormitories, or, in the more advanced colonies, to small houses in which some semblance of a family circle was maintained. Many people with severe epilepsy spent the greater part of their lives in such institutions. Unfortunately there is still a need for such long-term care. In the United Kingdom there are approximately 2000 people with epilepsy in the former colonies, now called centres for epilepsy, and perhaps another 3000 in other types of residential accommodation supported by local government.

An intriguing fact is that about one-sixth of those in the epilepsy centres have rare seizures — less often than once a year. Some of these epilepsies have, as it were, burnt themselves out, but the subject has been so long in the institution that he has no base or family circle to which he may return, and the centre is his much-loved home. The other explanation is that epilepsy, although a 'required' disorder for admission to the centres for epilepsy, may be in itself not a great problem – the major reasons for admission being associated impairment of intellect or major physical disability due to brain damage of which epilepsy is only one symptom. By and large, those in special centres for epilepsy have what has been termed 'epilepsy plus' – epilepsy plus some other major handicap.

The role of the former colonies has gradually changed over the years. First the word colony, with its implications of dependency and rule, has been dropped, and the name 'centre for epilepsy' has been adopted. Secondly, the centres have established much closer links with university departments of neurological sciences. Indeed much of the best research work in epilepsy in Europe emanates from the former colonies. Thirdly, the centres have taken a greater role in the assessment of patients with severe epilepsy, admitting them for neurological and occupational evaluation for a short period of a few weeks. Fourthly, they are more outward-looking in the employment of people with epilepsy. Sometimes the centre is used as a hostel to which the person with epilepsy who can almost, but not quite, manage on his own can return at night.

All this activity does mean that the primary role for which the colonies were established – a sheltered residential home for those people with epilepsy unable to cope outside – is in danger of being submerged. I can always tell when this is happening to a centre, because my letter requesting admission for a patient receives a reply that the patient 'would not benefit' from residence in the centre. In a small proportion of cases, one has to accept that benefit is not likely to occur, and all that is wanted is a clean, quiet, and kind place to live.

8

Febrile convulsions

Febrile convulsions are distinct from epilepsy, but bear an uneasy kinship to it. A febrile convulsion is a seizure – a paroxysmal discharge of cerebral neurones. Why, therefore, the distinction?

First of all, febrile convulsions are extremely frequent. A number of studies have shown that at least 3 per cent of all children have one or more febrile convulsions in the course of their development. They are rare below the age of six months, and above the age of five years, and most frequent between the ages of about 12 to 18 months. There is nothing very remarkable about the convulsion itself. It is like a grand mal attack (page 15) occurring in a little person.

As in the case of epileptic seizures, many factors interact to 'cause' or precipitate a febrile convulsion. As their name implies, they are always associated with fever, though this fever need not be particularly high. It seems to be the rate at which the temperature rises, rather than the final level, which is important in precipitating the convulsion. It is probable that many convulsions are associated with an otherwise unimportant viral infection. The convulsion may occur during the viraemia – that is to say, the stage during which viruses are replicating and circulating through the organs.

Genetic factors are also important in the causation of febrile convulsions. Twin studies have shown that if one of identical twins has a febrile convulsion, then the other has an 80 per cent chance of having a febrile convulsion. A non-identical twin or sibling of a child who has had a febrile convulsion has about a 25 per cent chance of having a febrile convulsion, a chance several times higher than the chances for the population of children as a whole. From such studies it is

believed that susceptibility to febrile convulsions is transmitted as a dominant gene.

There is some evidence that pre-existing structural changes
in the brain are, as in epilepsy, also relevant in the genesis
of febrile convulsions. Some children who convulse have
previously shown minor abnormalities of social and motor
development, possibly indicative of sub-clinical cerebral
lesions. In such children, therefore, a febrile convulsion
may call attention to a pre-existing developmental defect.
Years later, it may then be impossible to sort out those
neurological symptoms and signs due to factors which
preceded the convulsion, and those which are due to the
effects of the convulsion itself (page 35).

Many parents believe for a short and horrifying period
that their child is dying during the attack. What should they
do? As in the case of grand mal seizures, most attacks terminate spontaneously, within a minute or two, long before the
family doctor can arrive. Nevertheless, for reasons discussed
below, it is essential that further attacks are prevented. The
child should be uncovered, and sponged with tepid water to
bring his temperature down. A small oral dose of aspirin (60
mg per year of age — a fragment representing about a quarter
of an adult tablet will do) will also help.

If the family doctor finds the child still convulsing when
he arrives, then this is a medical emergency, and he must
terminate the attack as soon as possible. Diazepam (Valium)
is the best drug — though this may surprise some who think
of it as a panacea for anxious housewives. Ideally, the dose
should be given intravenously, but few family doctors, or
even paediatricians, are capable of giving an intravenous
injection into a convulsing infant in a poorly lit bedroom in
the middle of the night! The drug is perfectly well absorbed
from the rectum, and the ease and rapidity of rectal administration more than compensates for the abrupt effect of
intravenous injection. The rectal dose is 0.5 mg per kg body
weight.

Why do I place such stress on rapid termination of a

Febrile convulsions

febrile convulsion? During a convulsion, the normal movements of respiration are interrupted, and so less oxygen enters the blood circulating through the lungs. At the same time the enormous metabolic demands for oxygen from rapidly discharging neurones and convulsing muscles depletes the arterial oxygen content even further. Some tissues, in the absence of oxygen, use alternative pathways of metabolism, which results in the accumulation of acid metabolites in the blood. The imbalance between oxygen supply and oxygen demand of cerebral neurones may lead to irreversible damage to these neurones, particularly in the region of the hippocampus in the temporal lobe of the brain. In later life, the scarred hippocampus may evolve to become a focus from which arise temporal lobe epileptic seizures. If convulsions are very severe and prolonged, and predominantly unilateral, the child may be left with permanent weakness and partial failure of growth of the opposite limbs — a hemiplegia — and epilepsy.

Such an outcome is very unusual, but parents will want to know two things — will their child have further febrile convulsions, and will he develop epilepsy in later life?

The prognosis with regard to further febrile convulsions depends upon the age at which the first convulsion occurred, the sex of the child, and the family history. Girls under the age of 13 months stand a greater than one in two chance of having a further febrile convulsion, whilst the corresponding figure for boys is only one in three. The chances of recurrence become very much less at greater ages of first occurrence. The recurrence rate is only about 2 per cent if the first convulsion occurred after the age of three years.

Faced with these high chances of recurrence, in early infancy at least, parents will ask what they can do to prevent further febrile convulsions. It is no good giving oral anticonvulsant drugs at the start of a feverish illness, as the establishment of therapeutic blood levels takes too long. It is certainly worth making sure that the child is not overdressed for his environment, as he may be unable to lose the excess body heat generated by his infectious illness. Many children are grossly overdressed for the modern centrally heated house. The only reliable form of prevention, however, is to give long-term phenobarbitone to children at risk. This has been shown clearly to be effective in reducing the chances of subsequent febrile convulsions, though surprisingly phenytoin is not effective. Recent studies have suggested that sodium valproate may work, and if this is confirmed, we could avoid the side-effects of phenobarbitone, which are so common in young children (page 96). The present consensus is that all children who have their first febrile convulsion under the age of 13 months, and older children with a family history of febrile convulsions, should receive daily prophylactic medication until the age of three years.

What is the prognosis for the occurrence of later non-febrile seizures — that is to say of epilepsy? This depends greatly upon the age at which the febrile convulsion occurs, the duration of the convulsion, the presence of focal features during the convulsion (for example, convulsions effecting only one side of the body), and the presence of evidence of disturbance of development indicating pre-existing neurological abnormality. In a large prospective study of over 50 000 children carried out by the National Institute of Neurological and Communicative Disorders and Strokes in the United States, the incidence of febrile convulsions was 3.1 per cent, and the recurrence rate 32 per cent. By the time that the children had reached the age of seven years, more than one non-febrile seizure (i.e. epilepsy) had developed in 0.5 per cent of those who had *never* had a febrile convulsion, and in four times as many — 2 per cent — of those who *had* had a febrile convulsion. Children who had had prolonged or focal febrile convulsions, with evidence of pre-existing impaired development were eight times more likely to develop epilepsy by the age of seven years than children with simple febrile convulsions, and 18 times more likely than children who had never had a febrile convulsion at all.

These figures show that one cannot deny the relation

Febrile convulsions

between febrile convulsions and epilepsy. However, the parents of a child with one uncomplicated convulsion can be assured that the chances of subsequent epilepsy developing are very low — that the child has about 98 chances out of 100 of reaching the age of seven years without the occurrence of non-febrile seizures.

Finally, before leaving febrile convulsions on this optimistic note, we must remember that occasionally a convulsion with fever may be the manifestation of a highly important and dangerous illness such as meningitis. If there is any doubt about the matter at all, it is best for a doctor to do a lumbar puncture. This is a trivial procedure in the hands of an experienced doctor, and it is better to be safe than sorry.

There is no point in doing an electroencephalogram after a febrile convulsion, except in so far as a focal abnormality may prove to be an indicator of the subsequent development of epilepsy.

9

The promise of the future

The ideal management of any illness is to prevent its occurrence in the first place. What are the possibilities of preventing epilepsy?

Better obstetric care during pregnancy and childbirth will reduce the numbers of those suffering severe neurological damage and epilepsy due to birth trauma, but in developed countries such tragedies are fortunately already uncommon. Meningitis in early childhood may still be overlooked, as a young infant may not exhibit the classic sign of stiffness of the neck. Greater awareness of this point may save a few children developing post-meningitic epilepsy. In numerical terms, however, far more cases of epilepsy will be prevented by the prophylactic treatment of recurrent febrile convulsions (page 146), now coming into widespread use. Unfortunately, however, hippocampal scarring leading to subsequent epilepsy may be sustained in the very first febrile convulsion. After infancy, the most easily preventable cause of epilepsy is cranial trauma due to road traffic or industrial accidents. The requirement (in Great Britain) that motorcyclists wear crash helmets, and industrial workers protective headgear, will, hopefully, soon be followed by regulations requiring the wearing of seat-belts for car occupants. Cranial and facial injuries are very substantially reduced by such restraints.

I hope that no future society considers a return to attempts to eradicate epilepsy by the practice of eugenics. Except in the case of the rare specific genetic disorders, such as tuberose sclerosis, in which epilepsy is but one feature of a diffuse brain disease, even counselling against procreation would be, in my view, unjustifiable. The vast majority of

148

The promise of the future

those with epilepsy have children without epilepsy (page 33).

Finally, there is no early prospect of preventing cerebral tumours, or the epilepsy resulting from them.

It seems probable, therefore, that there will always be a considerable number of people who develop seizures. What more can be done to stop seizures, or at least to control them?

The most likely improvements in control will result from further development in the pharmaceutical industry, hand in hand with basic research in the neurosciences. Not everyone believes that experiments on animals to benefit Man are justifiable, but if one does accept the present widespread use of animals in research, there are several models of epilepsy, ranging from rodents that convulse on exposure to a loud sound, to baboons from West Senegal that display genetically determined photosensitive epilepsy. Given animal models, there are enormous possibilities for biological, and in particular biochemical, research into the processes that occur during a seizure. Founded on this research, even better drugs will surely be introduced in the future. It is unlikely that there will be a single dramatic advance to parallel the introduction in 1967 of L-dopa in the treatment of Parkinson's disease. Progress is more likely to occur by the gradual accretion of new knowledge. There are journals, such as *Epilepsia,* devoted to publication of the results of the best research in epilepsy. There are also regular international meetings of those interested in epilepsy, so any real advance will be rapidly disseminated throughout the world.

The lot of those with epilepsy would be greatly improved, even if their seizures continued, if others — especially employers — showed greater understanding of their intermittent disability. The most probable benefit for the present generation of those with epilepsy is likely to result from such increased tolerance, rather than from any dramatic advances in treatment. Tolerance depends upon understanding the facts about epilepsy. I hope this book will help.

Appendix. Associations for those with epilepsy

Patients with many sorts of chronic illnesses or disabilities, and their relatives, have banded themselves together into self-help associations. Randomly chosen examples include the Multiple Sclerosis Society, the Muscular Dystrophy Association, the American Association for the Hard of Hearing, and the Association to Combat Huntingdon's Disease. The aim of all such associations is to raise funds to foster scientific research into the illness, to provide mutual help and practical advice to families newly faced with the illness, and to educate the public into the difficulties facing those with the illness and inform the public how they may best help.

The first 'National Association for the Study of Epilepsy and the Care and Treatment of the Epileptic' was founded in New York in 1898. Nine years later the first meeting of International League Against Epilepsy took place. Various vicissitudes including two World Wars and a chronic lack of finance kept activity at a fairly low ebb until the 1950s, when the number of clinical neurophysiologists and neurologists interested in epilepsy expanded. Most developed countries now contain either an independent epilepsy association, or a branch of the International League, now known as Epilepsy International.

The aims of the British Epilepsy Association, for example, founded in 1950, are to offer advice and information to those with epilepsy on the domestic management of the condition, on schooling, on careers and employment, on life insurance and on welfare rights due under various National Insurance provisions. Such information is offered by letter, telephone calls, or by the distribution of excellent leaflets. The Association has been extremely active in raising funds through Action for Epilepsy groups now functioning in about 80 areas in the United Kingdom. Money has been raised not only specifically for research, but also for the purchase of a large country house which is used as a holiday centre for children with epilepsy, and also provides administrative headquarters for the Association far from the rocketing rents of Central London.

Appendix

The British Epilepsy Association is also active in its attempt to educate those without epilepsy, in a long drawn-out attempt to remove the misconceptions and fallacies about seizures, and to dispel the apparent stigma still attaching to the diagnosis. The Education Department of the Association is very happy to provide speakers at meetings organized by, for example, students at Teacher Training Colleges, or members of other voluntary associations. Literature, slides, and films are available for such meetings.

Membership of the Association is currently £5.00 per year, and for this members receive a free copy of the journal *Epilepsy News*, published quarterly, up-to-date information about all aspects of epilepsy, free advice and counselling service, and automatic accident insurance. The address of the Association is:

The British Epilepsy Association,
The National Centre for Social Aspects of Epilepsy,
Crowthorne House, Bagshotte,
New Wokingham Road,
Wokingham, Berkshire RG11 3AY,
England.
Tel. 03446 3122

I have written about the British Epilepsy Association, because that is the Association with which I have most contact. Organizations elsewhere in the world are listed on page 152.

Readers are earnestly encouraged to join their national epilepsy association. The individual membership fee is not vast, but when multiplied some tens of thousandfold useful sums of money are raised for further research and education. Newly joined members will be put in touch with their local Action Group or Chapter, or encouraged to begin one if there is no such local focus of activity in their own community. The strength of local groups lies in the opportunity for personal contact, so that subjects newly diagnosed as having epilepsy may talk through their problems, which other members have successfully overcome. The presence of a local group encourages those who have concealed their epilepsy to come forward and, by social contact, relieve themselves of the self-imposed isolation that the burden of secrecy has engendered. Those who have, on account of their epilepsy, categorized themselves as second-rate citizens, may gain new concepts of their potential for leadership by joining in the administration of the

151

local group. Finally there is the very real point that local people know local employers, and personal introduction is about the best way of getting a job in any walk of life.

Epilepsy associations worldwide

Australia (there is no national association in Australia)

Epilepsy Foundation of Victoria
Kintore Epilepsy Centre
181/182 Burke Road
Camberwell 3124
Victoria

Epilepsy Association of Queensland
Room 438,
Fifth Floor,
Pennys Bldg.,
210 Queen Street,
Brisbane,
Queensland 4000

Epilepsy Association of South Australia
Memorial Hospital
Pennington Terrace
North Adelaide, S. Australia 5006

Epilepsy Association of Tasmania
P.O. Box 421
Sandy Bay
Tasmania, Aus. 7005

Western Australia Epilepsy Association
14, Bagot Road
Subiaco 6008
W. Australia

Epileptic Welfare Association
158 Pacific Highway
North Sidney, N.S.W. 2060

Canada (although Epilepsy Canada exists on paper, there is no national association in Canada as yet)

Appendix

Quebec Epilepsy Association (Epilepsie Montreal)
493, ouest, rue Sherbrooke
Montreal, Quebec H3A 1B6

Epilepsy Association-Metro Toronto
214 King Street, West
Suite 214
Toronto, Ontario M5H 1K4

Epilepsy Association of Calgary
2422–5 Avenue, N.W.
Calgary, Alberta T2N 0T2

Edmonton Epilepsy Association
308 Robt. Armstrong Bldg.
10012 Jasper Avenue
Edmonton, Alberta T5J 1RJ

British Columbia Epilepsy Society
1721 Richmond Road
Victoria, B.C. V8R 4P9

Ontario Epilepsy Association
90 Eglington Avenue, East
Suite 405
Toronto, Ontario M4P 1A6

India

The Indian Epilepsy Association
251, Dr. Dadabhoy Naoroji Road
Fort, Bombay 400 001

Ireland

Irish Epilepsy Association
23 Dawson Street
Dublin 2, Eire

New Zealand

New Zealand Epilepsy Association
P.O. Box 683
Hamilton, N.Z.

Epilepsy: the facts

Scotland

Scottish Epilepsy Association
48, Govan Road
Glasgow GS1 1JL

Epilepsy Association of Edinburgh and SE Region
13, Guthrie Street
Edinburgh EH1 1JG

South Africa

South African National Epilepsy League (SANEL)
P.O. Box 4197
201–203 Barclays Bank Bldg
Church Square, Pretoria

U.S.A.

Epilepsy Foundation of America
Suite 406
1828 'L' Street NW
Washington D.C., 20036

(N.B. there are hundreds of independent state and local bodies dealing with epilepsy. EFA will advise on what is available in each area.)

Index

Index

156

Index

medulla oblongata 17, Fig. 1(b)
memory 5, 35
meningitis 39, 51, 148
meningioma 38, Plate 1, 2
menstruation 45
micturition syncope 59
migraine 63
mobility allowance 130-1
Mogadon, *see* nitrazepam
myoclonic jerks 17, 48-9, 64
myoclonic seizures 21, 74, Fig. 12
Mysoline, *see* primidone

narcolepsy 63
neurofibromatosis 30, 79
neurologist
    actions of 54-7
    definition of v
    referral to 52
neurone 1, 4, 5, 14, 15, 79
night terrors 65
nitrazepam 86, 91

oligodendroglioma 38
Ospolot *see* sulthiame
overbreathing (hyperventilation) 66,
    72

partial seizure 17-21
    EEG in 71
petit mal 16, 24, 72
phenobarbitone 83, 87, 88, 89, 91,
    92, 94, 95, 96, 97, 98, 124
phenytoin 83, 87, 88, 89, 91, 93, 94,
    95, 96, 97, 98, 123
photic stimulation 74
photoconvulsive response 47
photosensitive epilepsy 47, 74, 149,
    Fig. 12
post-ictal
    amnesia 20, 25
    automatism 25
    confusion 16, 20, 25
    paresis 25
precipitants of seizures 43-48, 81
    alcohol 44
    drugs 46-7
    menstruation 45
    mood 45

sleep and lack of sleep 43
stress and worry 45
television 48
prednisone 102
pregnancy 97-8, 122-4
prejudice 119-20
prevalence 9, 11, 24
primary generalized epilepsy 13, 22,
    30-1
primidone 85, 88, 89, 90, 91, 93, 94,
    96, 125
prodrome 26
prognosis 110-14
psychiatric disorders 120-2

reflex epilepsy 47-8
research for the future 148-9
rigors 65
Rivotril, *see* clonazepam

salaam seizures, *see* infantile spasms
scan, *see* computed axial tomography
schools 125-6
seizure 4, 5, 6, 8
    absences,
        typical 16, 24, 72
        atypical 21
    adversive 19
    akinetic drop attacks 21
    anoxic 60
    apoplectic 8
    clonic 21
    differential diagnosis of 57-7
    epileptiform 9
    epileptoid 9
    first 50 *et seq.*
    focal 17
    grand mal 15-16, 24, 115-16
    infantile spasms 26, 102, 114
    investigation of 51-57, 67-80
    Jacksonian 19
    myoclonic 21, 74, Fig. 12
    nocturnal 44
    partial 13, 17-21, 71
    partial with secondary generaliz-
        ation 13
    petit mal 16, 24, 72
    petit mal variant 21
    precipitants of 43-8, 81

Index